The Mindfulness and Character Strengths Workbook

About the Author

Ryan M. Niemiec (pronounced "knee-mick"), PsyD, is a leading international figure in the education, science, and practice of character strengths that are found in all human beings. Dr. Niemiec is Chief Science and Education Officer of the renown Values in Action (VIA) Institute on Character, a nonprofit organization in Cincinnati, Ohio, that leads the global advancement of the science of character strengths. He has been at the center of this work, positively impacting many millions of people.

Ryan is also an award-winning psychologist, certified coach, annual instructor at the University of Pennsylvania, and a member of the special guest faculty at five coaching and positive psychology institutes. Ryan received the Distinguished Early Career Award from the American Psychological Association and was awarded Fellow of the International Positive Psychology Association (IPPA), also serving on their Council of Advisors. He is cofounder and president of the Spirituality/Meaning Division of IPPA.

Ryan has authored 14 books, over 100 academic papers, and several hundred user-friendly articles (his blog on *Psychology Today* is called What Matters Most?). His books include the bestselling consumer book *The Power of Character Strengths* and books on stress management, strengths in teens, positive movies, and strengths for disabilities/abilities. He is also the author of the two leading practitioner-focused books in positive psychology – *Character Strengths Interventions* and *Mindfulness and Character Strengths*. The latter book contains the evidenced-based program he founded, mindfulness-based strengths practice (MBSP), now used by practitioners and researchers in more than 50 countries. He created an MBSP Certification in 2021, the first character strengths certification program. Ryan has led hundreds of mindfulness-based program sessions for clinical and lay audiences and has led the MBSP program in particular over 20 times.

Ryan cofounded Blooming Strengths Sangha, an open, global mindfulness and character strengths community that focuses on practices, experiences, and mindful-living community building. His lineage name, in the tradition of Thich Nhat Hanh, is Fullest Breath of the Heart, and he is an aspirant for ordination in the Order of Interbeing.

Ryan lives in Cincinnati with his wife and three young, zestful children. His highest strengths are hope, love, honesty, fairness, spirituality, curiosity, and appreciation of beauty. In his leisure time, he practices tai chi, plays tennis, basketball, and chess, and is a zealot of Michigan State University athletics, a collector of vintage and rare Pez dispensers. He also engages in creative writing and in building communities in mindfulness and character strengths.

The Mindfulness and Character Strengths Workbook

Ryan M. Niemiec, PsyD

Library of Congress of Congress Cataloging in Publication information for the accompanying therapists' guide
Mindfulness and Character Strengths: A Practical Guide to MBSP is available via the Library of Congress Marc Database
under the Library of Congress Control Number 2023938679

Library and Archives Canada Cataloguing in Publication

Title: The mindfulness and character strengths workbook / Ryan M. Niemiec, PsyD.
Names: Niemiec, Ryan M., author.
Description: Includes bibliographical references.
Identifiers: Canadiana (print) 20230447805 | Canadiana (ebook) 20230447953 | ISBN 9780889376380
  (softcover) | ISBN 9781616766382 (PDF) | ISBN 9781613346389 (EPUB)
Subjects: LCSH: Meditation—Problems, exercises, etc. | LCSH: Attention—Problems, exercises, etc. |
  LCSH: Character—Problems, exercises, etc. | LCSH: Self-actualization (Psychology)—Problems,
  exercises, etc. | LCGFT: Problems and exercises.
Classification: LCC BF637.M4 N534 2023 | DDC 158.1/2—dc23

© 2024 by Hogrefe Publishing
www.hogrefe.com

Cover image: iStock.com/Sylvia Becerra Gonzalez

PUBLISHING OFFICES

USA: Hogrefe Publishing Corporation, 44 Merrimac Street, Suite 207, Newburyport, MA 01950
                Phone (978) 255 3700; E-mail customersupport@hogrefe.com

EUROPE: Hogrefe Publishing GmbH, Merkelstr. 3, 37085 Göttingen, Germany
                Phone +49 551 99950 0, Fax +49 551 99950 111; E-mail publishing@hogrefe.com

SALES & DISTRIBUTION

USA: Hogrefe Publishing, Customer Services Department,
                30 Amberwood Parkway, Ashland, OH 44805
                Phone (800) 228 3749, Fax (419) 281 6883; E-mail customersupport@hogrefe.com

UK: Hogrefe Publishing, c/o Marston Book Services Ltd., 160 Eastern Ave.,
                Milton Park, Abingdon, OX14 4SB
                Phone +44 1235 465577, Fax +44 1235 465556; E-mail direct.orders@marston.co.uk

EUROPE: Hogrefe Publishing, Merkelstr. 3, 37085 Göttingen, Germany
                Phone +49 551 99950 0, Fax +49 551 99950 111; E-mail publishing@hogrefe.com

OTHER OFFICES

CANADA: Hogrefe Publishing Corporation, 82 Laird Drive, East York, Ontario M4G 3V1

SWITZERLAND: Hogrefe Publishing, Länggass-Strasse 76, 3012 Bern

Printed and bound in the USA
ISBN 978-0-88937-638-0 (print) · ISBN 978-1-61676-638-2 (PDF) · ISBN 978-1-61334-638-9 (EPUB)
http://doi.org/10.1027/00638-000

Gratitude

I am grateful there are authentic and meaning-filled organizations such as the two that are central to the creation of this book – the VIA Institute and Hogrefe Publishing – and the wonderful people that help these companies shine.

I deeply appreciate those who had a positive impact on the creation of this Workbook: Ruth Pearce, Breta Cooper, Kelly Aluise, Matthijs Steeneveld, Dandan Pang, Masaya Okamoto, Roger Bretherton, and Polina Beloborodova, hundreds of MBSP participants, and three MBSP Certification cohorts.

With thankfulness to my family, friends, and other colleagues, past and present. I acknowledge, with a sense of interbeing, that none of what I do is alone and all I do is a culmination of countless experiences and efforts of you and others across numerous generations. From an immediate perspective, I bow to my Mom, Dad, siblings, wife, and three children. Love to "R4 x M" always...

Dedication

I once had this conversation with a wise person: I asked them,
"Of all the great teachings out there, what is the best practice you would recommend?"
"There is only one practice that matters," they said.
"Really?! Which one?" I asked.
"The one you do."

I dedicate this book to my wise teachers, past and present, all who reside in my present.

One of my wise teachers is my son Ryland who reminds me that mindfulness should be playful and enjoyable. He dislikes brushing his teeth so to improve the experience, one morning when I was helping him brush I asked him to take a slow inhale and exhale while brushing. After the inhale, which he found a bit odd, he exclaimed out of nowhere, "Chicken!" Now, hundreds of times later, as I support him in brushing, we take an inbreath, exclaim "Chicken!", roar with laughter, and continue brushing.

This is true mindful teeth-brushing. May I always learn from you, my gentle and loving boy, Ryland.

Contents

Preface

A student asked a Zen master, "What is the most important thing?" and the Zen master responded with, "The most important thing is to remember the most important thing."

With mindfulness (your curious and open awareness) and character strengths (the best, core parts of you), you always have the most important things within you. As you learn, practice, and discuss these areas, you'll take notice of your kindness and fairness, you'll feel more gratitude and hope, you'll uncover your bravery and perseverance, connect with your honesty and humility, and readily use your curiosity and spirituality. You'll see that mindfulness and character strengths are pathways to the most important thing, and they are the most important thing itself.

What is your "most important thing?" For me, it is my family. Is family not a manifestation of our love, kindness, forgiveness, social intelligence, humor, gratitude, and mindful attention? For someone else, the most important thing might be work productivity or contributing to others. Is that not a manifestation of perseverance, zest, self-regulation, hope, kindness, creativity, and mindful effort?

Mindfulness and character strengths are within all of us, and they are for all of us – regardless of age, gender, occupation, education level, country of origin, beliefs, and personality type. The many benefits of mindfulness and of character strengths are captured in the graphic above. Modern science points to these two overarching buckets of benefit – the uplift to our well-being and the facing, coping with, or overcoming of adversity.

Within each, there are many streams of benefit such as enhancing happiness, inner peace, meaning in life, improved health, better work performance, and more positive relationships in the well-being bucket. And in the adversity bucket, there is stress management, illness coping, reducing relationship conflict, and handling anxiety, sadness, and anger. Both mindfulness and character strengths help with well-being and with adversity. Imagine what bringing them together can do!

I wrote this Workbook for two main reasons: One, there are no available books for the general public on the integration of character strengths and mindfulness. Two, I heard over and over again from practitioners leading *mindfulness-based strengths practice* (MBSP) sessions that they needed a user-friendly book for their MBSP students, employees, and clients. This is that Workbook to serve both purposes!

Therefore, this Workbook is a stand-alone resource for anyone. If you are not part of an MBSP program or group, then you might view this Workbook as a guidebook supporting you. View the Workbook as containing your own personal *self-development sessions*! You might take 1 week per session (give or take) and really dig into your personal growth, and engage in the explorations, activities, and suggestions in the worksheets. May this Workbook be like a peaceful yet challenging friend, supporting you on your life journey.

And, this Workbook can (and should) be used as a companion for those participating in MBSP groups or individual MBSP sessions or workshops. The facilitator of MBSP will naturally have the MBSP manual found in *Mindfulness and Character Strengths* (2nd edition), which was written for practitioners who lead MBSP programs and who study the integration of mindfulness and character strengths. MBSP facilitators will often recommend that participants attain this Workbook you have in your hands. You'll be able to follow along in this Workbook session-by-session with the 8-week program of MBSP. You have the activities, worksheets, home practice suggestions, and more (!). It is all right here, and I hope it will help you make the most of the MBSP experience, help you connect with others in your MBSP community, and support you on your life journey.

If you are interested in learning more about what MBSP is, then you can read Reading Activity 1.1 in Session 1.

The MBSP program is being used across the globe, having reached every continent (except Antarctica), with an estimated hundreds of MBSP facilitators (in-person and virtual) from all walks of life – coaches, psychologists, business professionals, human resources specialists, teachers, parents, and scientists. They report that participants experience large benefits from the program. The latest science is showing their findings are not unique to them. When MBSP has been compared with the most popular mindfulness-based program on the planet (mindfulness-based stress reduction/MBSR), MBSP has come out as stronger every time.

All of this means you have arrived at the right place. Whether you are hoping to manage stress and problems better, are seeking growth and self-improvement, or are helping others to do the same, this Workbook will be an important and supportive tool for your journey.

May this Workbook brighten your journey, lighten your tension, and deepen the joy and meaning of your life.

Ryan M. Niemiec
July 2023

Introduction:
Beginning Your Journey

Smile, breathe, and go slowly.

Thich Nhat Hanh

A story to remember

I was in a Zoom meeting with a group of 20 people – all cameras on. It was a social gathering, but the topic had grown serious – one of the members had an untreatable cancer and was speaking about how he was coping with his situation. The mood was somber, and all of the participants were attending closely to the man as he slowly shared his experiences, with a heaviness in his voice. Then, unbeknownst to me the head of Maya, my 7-year-old daughter, popped up behind mine on the screen. She must have picked the lock on my office door and crept in! At an angle, she smiled widely and curiously at the many faces of the group. I immediately attempted to *verbally* guide her to the door, while simultaneously listening to the man sharing his suffering, but she responded by breaking out into one of her new dance moves and starting to sing (thankfully, my computer was muted). My words were futile to my dancing daughter, as were my feigned attempts to continue listening closely to my friend.

As I started to stand up to physically guide Maya to the door, he spoke to us: "And I appreciate the young new member of our meeting," and he began to laugh. Smiles began to appear throughout the group. "I needed that levity right now. Sometimes it is just too much always talking about my cancer." He paused, with the group hanging on every word. "This little girl's curiosity…and humor…and zest – that's what I needed to see. That's what I want for myself too, right now. Thank you, thank you."

Your Journey Begins Now

Life can appear messy and unpredictable. Often there are no perfect responses – only responses. However, we have tools to help us. We have tools to make our lives better and the lives around us better.

The pursuit of a happier and more meaningful life is vitally important to people in today's world. The challenges, stressors, and obstacles to building greater well-being, better relationships, more work productivity, and a higher purpose are too numerous to count.

New research shows that practices with mindfulness and character strengths offer some of the best pathways for you to not only unleash greater fulfillment and live your best life but also improve in managing your problems, stressors, conflicts, and other typical life adversities. This Workbook will help you boost your mindfulness and your character strengths. You'll learn ways to catch your mind wandering and being distracted, and become more mindful at home, work, and in your relationships.

You'll learn ways to become more tuned into your best qualities – your character strengths – and how to explore and use them not only more frequently but more wisely. Along the journey, you'll practice the many ways to weave together both, in your daily life.

If you smile, breathe, and go slowly, you'll soon see, mindfulness and character strengths work hand in glove.

Why Bring Mindfulness and Character Strengths Together?

You will soon dive into mindful awareness practices and character strengths practices. The latest science shows that mindfulness practices help you feel happier and more positive, as well as give you a strong boost in your coping skills to deal with stress and other life difficulties. Research suggests the same is true for practices involving your character strengths. But what are the benefits of bringing the two together and developing them in unison?

Here is a summary of the importance of bringing mindfulness and character strengths together.

Mindfulness without character strengths is deflated. Many people who engage in mindfulness or meditation practices quickly lose focus, find their interest wanes, and hit so many detours that they give up. Character strengths provide energy, substance, and direction to the practice of mindfulness. Strengths help you to start and then maintain a practice of mindful walking, of mindful listening, or of mindful meditation. They lead you to get the most out of mindfulness practices.

Character strengths without mindfulness are hollow. The mindless use of our character strengths is commonplace (think of an automatic "Thank you" or "I love you" that we offer without even thinking about it, without conscious use of your character strengths of gratitude and love). At times we may speak in ways that are superficial and unconscious, and at other times judgmental or unbalanced. As mindfulness is applied to character strengths, however, use of them becomes focused, like an archer directing an arrow to a bull's-eye. Your relationships are enhanced. Meaning is deepened. Fulfillment is reached.

Mindfulness, Character Strengths, and You!

In this Workbook, you will:

- Discover and deeply understand your inner capacity to be mindful and to see and use your character strengths.
- Identify your signature strengths, overused strengths, and underused strengths, and how to improve each.
- Examine ways you can connect character strengths and mindfulness in your life to enhance your well-being and manage problems.
- Learn new ways to apply mindfulness to your character strengths and, in turn, to apply your character strengths to daily mindful living.
- Build your mindfulness/character strengths toolbox by gathering numerous practical strategies that can be used throughout your life.
- Take immediate action with your character strengths and mindfulness.

A wonderful way to grow your self-awareness is to explore your mindfulness and character strengths from multiple angles. This Workbook guides you through doing that by offering a variety of questions, activities, and opportunities to reflect on your thoughts, feelings, ideas, actions, and behaviors. In the process of connecting the dots, you can formulate a plan to bring your strengths and mindfulness into your everyday life.

This Workbook will help you explore your mindfulness and character strengths and support you with reflection questions. Let's try it now:

? What got you interested in mindfulness and/or character strengths?

_____

_____

_____

_____

? What excites you about these topics?

_____

_____

_____

_____

? What brought you to this particular set of self-awareness tools?

_____

_____

_____

_____

? What do you hope to accomplish by engaging with this workbook?

_____

_____

_____

_____

Your journey toward elevating your mindfulness and character strengths will be fluid – new ideas, activities, conversations, and meditations will come and go. Each has the potential to impact you positively. Allow yourself to be open to the possibilities as you navigate the terrain that is within you.

You'll discover that turning to your mindfulness and your character strengths is always an option you can take in life to help you reach greater fulfillment, fortify your personal relationships, and achieve the goals that matter most to you. Enjoy!

Working to combine and build mindfulness and character strengths is an ongoing journey.

How to use this workbook mindfully

1. Start with Session 1 and work through the material sequentially.
2. Give yourself about 1 week per session. You may find that longer or shorter spans are called for per session, so do what works best for you.
3. Following the reading and reflection questions in each session, you'll find a tracking sheet to self-monitor your experience during the week and highlight the week's audio meditations (Audio Tracks; available online to purchasers of the book, see p. 145f. on how to access this material) and practice activities. These activities have been designed to build on the lessons from the chapter and will help you start, expand, and deepen your practice of mindfulness and character strengths.
4. At the end of each Session there is a summary (Your MBSP Toolbox) of the key insights and the science on the topic at hand, as well as questions for exploration, pearls of wisdom, and the MBSP tools.
5. For those completing a MBSP program with a practitioner, they will provide guidance as to when to ideally complete the activities. For some MBSP groups, the MBSP practitioner (facilitator, leader) will suggest to do the session's reading/reflecting/activities prior to the group session and for others it will be suggested to start them after the session occurs, while for others it will be a flexible mix of these approaches. The timing will reflect the MBSP leader's teaching style, the timing during the week the live session occurs, and other factors.
6. Be patient. Use perseverance to let your mindfulness and character strengths develop and expand.
7. Share your experiences. You will reinforce your insights by discussing them with others.

Session 1:
Mindfulness and Autopilot

There is another world. And it is in this one.

Paul Eluard

A story to remember

There was a quiet entomologist who attended a mindfulness-based strengths practice (MBSP) program. He described himself as a loner and was clear to say, "I study bugs, not people." In the first session he explained that when he does talk, he talks a lot, noting this probably had something to do with his difficulty relating to others and filling up the silence due to his uncertainty around people. He explained one of his intentions in MBSP was to develop more mindful speech, saying, "I want to speak less, listen better, and most of all, understand more." As the group dynamic unfolded, he flowered. Bringing mindfulness to his autopilot speaking and hearing others describe his creativity, kindness, and fairness, would often bring him to tears. These were parts of himself that were always there, but he was now opening up to them. He heard stories from group members about showing love for their father, and he wished he had shown more love to his father before he passed away. He focused on understanding this – understanding himself and his loss and suffering and also understanding the group member's experience. As his journey progressed, he summarized his experience as – "Perhaps I don't study bugs or people, I study the interconnection among all forms of life, and I wish to continue my understanding of those connections."

This now-curious entomologist took great care to attend to his autopilot mind and grow in mindfulness and strengths, resulting in deep and ongoing personal impact. This is possible for each one of us.

What Is Mindfulness?

What comes to mind when you hear the word "mindfulness"? Write your responses in the space provided below each question.

? What is mindfulness?

_____

_____

_____

_____

? How would you describe mindfulness to someone?

_____

_____

_____

_____

? How is mindfulness practiced?

_____

_____

_____

_____

_____

There are many useful definitions and ideas about mindfulness. One of the best (and strongest, from a scientific perspective) is that mindfulness has two core parts:

1. **Self-regulation:** This means you take control of what you put your attention on. Are you deciding to focus on inhaling and exhaling, on your child's face, the computer screen in front of you, the taste of your soup, or the feeling of cool air against your skin? When you deliberately put your attention on something, that is one part of your mindfulness. _This is the "what" of mindfulness._

2. **Curiosity, openness, acceptance:** This means you open your mind to whatever you are focusing on – to be interested and open to it. This attitude also involves acceptance of what is happening in the moment, whether that's stress, a positive feeling, or boredom – not trying to change it, not trying to criticize it, but simply accepting the reality in this particular moment, putting your curiosity to work. _This is the "how" of mindfulness._

Did either of these elements come up in your written descriptions? If not, you can begin to weave these two parts into your thinking about mindfulness and when you are practicing "being more mindful." As you go about your day, you might say to yourself, "I'm going to take greater control of what I focus on and I'm going to be curious and accepting of this difficulty I'm thinking about."

This way of understanding mindfulness can be applied to anything we are doing – working, driving, scrolling on social media, showering, crying, laughing, running, shopping. At any time, you can take control of your attention and focus it on your fingers as they make contact with your device's screen, for example, or with the softness of the fur of your pet. Your approach can be one of openness and curiosity – for example, being curious about the movement of your legs as you exercise and open to the words of your colleague as you listen.

In this way, mindfulness is a form of meditation ("meditation" is a specific practice, usually involving focused attention, that is used to cultivate greater mindfulness). You can learn to follow your in-breath and out-breath while sitting calmly in a chair. And mindfulness can be meditation in motion when you attend to your feet and posture and the pacing of your strides when you walk. You can mindfully eat a bite of food using all of your senses.

With mindfulness, you have the opportunity to experience your life deliberately and completely.

Despite the simplicity of this explanation, there is a lot of confusion about what mindfulness is, a lot of talk about "being in the present moment." And rightfully so, since research shows that a mindfulness practice helps people improve their well-being and manage their stress. As popular as mindfulness is in the current climate, however, there are still many misconceptions about it.

What Mindfulness Is Not

Mindfulness is not the same as a trance state, being in "flow," spiritual "oneness," or reciting mantras. It does not mean making your body totally calm and relaxed, being in a quiet place, sitting still, or giving up control of your mind. It does not have to involve a guru or wise person. Did any of those misconceptions come up in your answers to the questions earlier? If they did, that is normal. As you work through this Workbook, your understanding of mindfulness will evolve and you will reap the benefits of that.

A great way to start the process of expanding your understanding of mindfulness is to consider times when you are *not* mindful (which, for most of us, is most of the time). This common state of mind is referred to as *autopilot mind*. This occurs when we go through the motions of an activity without much awareness, not attending to the sights, smells, sounds, body language, emotions, thoughts, desires, and other stimuli within us and around us.

No doubt you can easily think of examples of being in autopilot mode, such as when you're making the bed, cooking a meal, walking the dog, or checking your social media account. Have you ever come to the end of your lunch only to realize you didn't taste a single bite? Or maybe you recall talking to a co-worker when your mind trailed off 30 seconds into their story, so you lost track of the details and didn't notice their body language and tone of voice. Or driving along for 45 minutes before you realize you hadn't been paying attention to *anything* – not the trees, the sky, the steering wheel, the buildings you passed, the air conditioner blowing – you were simply driving along on autopilot. The examples are virtually endless.

Coming to understand your autopilot mind – and how incredibly common (and normal) it is – can serve you well in appreciating mindfulness and finding your way back to the present moment when your attention wanes.

List three of your daily routines in which you are least mindful (most caught up in autopilot):

1. _____

2. _____

3. _____

Whether you wrote down brushing your teeth, shower-ing, shaving, making coffee, or driving to work, you can readily discover your autopilot mind. The mind is quick to wander off into thoughts, memories, previous conver-sations, and plans for the day. Often, the last thing we are focused on is the toothbrush, the soap, or the measuring spoon we're holding. Regarding the activities you just wrote down, can you relate to the idea of your mind on autopilot?

Before moving on to the "why" of mindfulness, there's one more important point to know about the "what" of mindfulness. Mindfulness does not mean to stay in the present moment. No person stays in the here and now. Rather, mindfulness is the *return* to the present moment. It's catching the mind when it wanders off and returning it back to the task at hand, back to your breathing, back to the person you're with, back to the colorful leaves on the trees around you. You might find this phrase useful: *Catch your autopilot mind, as soon as possible*, or *Catch AP-ASAP*, for short. Then return your mind to the present moment.

Why Does Mindfulness Matter?

Is it time to wake up?

Scores of studies show there are substantial benefits to waking yourself up with the practice of mindfulness. It ben-efits the brain and the immune system. It boosts our well-being, reduces our stress, and improves our social relation-ships. It helps people to lessen the impact of a wide range of medical and psychological disorders, and it leads them to feel more in control of managing their symptoms.

 DID YOU KNOW?

Research shows that when we think about ourselves, make decisions, and interact with others, we are doing these actions with lots of personal blind spots. We all have pockets of unawareness about who we are and how we are coming across to others. Research also shows that mindfulness can help overcome these blind spots (Carl-son, 2013).

Start a regular meditation practice (you'll learn about dif-ferent practices to try at the end of this session). Be curi-ous about what insights you might experience. Be open to seeing yourself in a clear way – strengths, struggles, and everything in between!

You Are Lucky

As we practice with mindfulness and observe our mind and body more and more each day, we become aware of a couple interesting realizations:

1. **We are lucky to have found mindfulness:** This sen-timent – if we allow it to sink in – becomes palpable on a feeling level, not just a concept level. This capacity within us – to notice and be present fully to what mat-ters most to us – is a capacity to be incredibly grateful for. The intention here is *not* to proclaim one is blessed, more lucky than others, or privileged. The capacity for mindfulness of oneself, of others, and of the world is for any human being to access and is not the sole occu-pation of a particular group of people, a particular kind of person, or relegated to certain beliefs, language, country, status, or ability. It is a capacity we can develop within and therefore improve ourselves.

2. **We do not have the luxury to be mindless:** You may notice more and more how precious your time is – and how limited it is. You probably want to make the most of your time and therefore be present with who and what is in front of you. You may take this sentiment fur-ther and say to yourself – how could I have the audac-ity to be mindless or go through life like an automaton when so many people cannot do what I can do (e.g., walk, hear, think deeply, work, eat without help, relate closely to others, and so forth)? How dare I take these for granted? While this is true, we want to be gentle, patient, and compassionate with ourselves as we prog-ress forward in our self-understanding and growth.

As we progress through this Workbook, we can make an effort to hold all of this together – our "luckiness," our self-gentleness, our eyes toward personal growth, and our compassion for others' suffering.

In addition to the science, on a practical level, mind-fulness "wakes us up" to life. We take a fresh look at what is happening within us and around us. Our tendency to just sleepwalk through the motions of life decreases, and our awareness and appreciation of life increases. When we recognize ourselves on autopilot, our mindfulness kicks into gear. As a result, we not only notice the posi-tives all around us and deepen our connections with oth-ers, but we more clearly and honestly assess our chal-lenges and difficulties, which affords us the ability to manage them better.

Waking Up

In other words, with mindfulness, we become present and active participants in the fullness of life – the ups, the downs, and the in-betweens. Mindfulness should be enjoyable – a mindful enjoyment as we cook, hug, sip tea, bike-ride, and bathe. But in order to know joy and experience joy, we must know and experience suffering. The two cannot be separated. When you suffer from something, you long for relief of suffering and the emergence of joy. And when you feel joy, you are also appreciating that you are not suffering. We can bring joy into our mindfulness practice.

Recall the quote that opens this chapter from a poet, Paul Eluard, who was best friends with Pablo Picasso nearly a century ago. The quote is a bit puzzling at first – another world? And it's in this one? As we develop our mindfulness and deepen our understanding and practice of mindfulness, we discover that Eluard is right. We see the colors, the brightness, the shapes, around us. We see ourselves more clearly. We see others in a different way, even though they were right in front of us all along. It's as if we are encountering a new world. Mindfulness helps us to touch that new world.

Essential Reminders to Develop a Mindfulness Practice

As you progress through this Workbook, you'll want to set up the formal practice of mindfulness, referred to as *meditation*. Meditation is a way for you to establish a solid foundation for using your mindfulness – and your character strengths. It helps you keep an active and healthy mind.

If you don't know where to start, then just start with consistency: Practice at the same time each day, for the same amount of time each day. Do this for a couple weeks and then evaluate your approach to see what's working and what's not. In this way, you will develop a habit. It is the consistency of the practice over time that increases the benefits for your brain, well-being, and stress. There are many theories and approaches to mindfulness, but if there's one thing that every teacher, researcher, practitioner, and author agrees on, it is that you need to *practice, practice, practice*.

Note that it's more important to take action doing something with mindfulness, however small, than to spend all your energy trying to force yourself to be mindful. Here are a few tips to help you jump in so you can begin acquiring the benefits of mindfulness.

1. **Start small.** Focus your attention on your in-breath and your out-breath as you sit in your favorite chair. When your mind wanders – and it will – bring your attention back to your breath. Choose an amount of time you are comfortable devoting each day. Maybe 3 minutes in the morning or 10 minutes before bed? Maybe a few minutes over your lunch break? You can always increase the time, so the most important thing is to pick a time and *just start*.
2. **Start easy.** What idea motivates you the most? To sit outside under your favorite tree and follow your breathing? To mindfully attend to your senses as you take your daily walk? To eat two pieces of food per day mindfully? Although many people start with mindful sitting and focusing on their breathing, you don't have to. Follow your highest motivation. Just remember that there's a big difference between "going for a walk" and "mindful walking," between "eating my food" and "mindful eating."
3. **Practice imperfectly.** Accept that you won't meditate perfectly, that you won't "be mindful" perfectly, and that you won't "stay" in the present moment. There is no perfection. There is no staying. There is only imperfection, making an effort, and then *returning* to the present moment.
4. **Enjoy mindfulness.** Through the good, bad, and the neutral, you can find enjoyment in being mindful. Don't be too serious! Be playful, smile, and breathe as you return to the present moment.

It's time to delve into some practices. The body-mindfulness meditation and practice activity (mindfulness of a routine activity) are two of the core practices this week that are designed to help you build upon the ideas discussed in this chapter. Engage in these each day to solidify your learnings and lay the groundwork for the next chapter. After about one week of practice, you'll be ready to move on to Session 2.

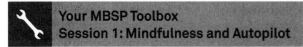

Your MBSP Toolbox
Session 1: Mindfulness and Autopilot

Key Insights

- The *what* of mindfulness is the self-regulation of your attention. This means you decide what you put your attention on (e.g., someone's smile, a sip of coffee, your inhale and exhale).

- The *how* of mindfulness is your mind's openness, curiousness, and acceptance to whatever you put your attention on (e.g., someone's smile, a sip of coffee, your inhale and exhale).

- When you are in *autopilot mind* you are in thinking mode – not attending to your senses, feelings, and inner experiences. This is a normal state of mind that is our default mode much of the time.

- You can learn to tap into *mindful mind* at any moment with *Catch AP-ASAP* (catching your autopilot mind, as soon as possible).

From the Science

- When we think about ourselves, make decisions, and interact with others, we have a number of gaps, biases, and personal blind spots. Research shows that mindfulness can help us overcome many of our personal blind spots (Carlson, 2013).

For Your Exploration

- When are you most prone to go into autopilot mind?
- When are you most prone to be awake (or in a mindful mind)?

Pearl of Wisdom

- You are lucky to have discovered mindfulness, this internal capacity that helps you to be present to what matters most to you in life. Therefore, we do not have the luxury to be walking through life chronically in autopilot.

Expand Your Toolbox

- Beginner's Mind Meditation (Audio Track 1): Eat one bite of food or drink one sip of water as if for the first time, using all of your senses.

- Mindfulness With a Routine Activity (Practice Activity 1.1): Consider a daily activity that you typically do on autopilot, lost in your thinking or distraction, and engage in that activity with mindfulness, giving it your full attention each day.

Mindfulness-Based Strengths Practice (MBSP)
Activities and Tracking Sheet: Session 1

Suggested Activities for This Week

- Beginner's Mind Activity (Audio Track 1). Listen to at least once.
- Body-Mindfulness Meditation (Audio Track 2). Practice ×1/day.
- Practice mindfulness with one routine activity each day (the same activity all week) and record your observations in Practice Worksheet 1.1.
- Look at Reading Activity 1.1. Overview of Mindfulness-Based Strengths Practice.
- Reflect on a You at Your Best experience (listen to Audio Track 3).
- Track your experiences on this sheet or in your journal.

Day & date	Type of practice & time length	Strengths used	Observations & comments
Monday Date:			
Tuesday Date:			
Wednesday Date:			
Thursday Date:			
Friday Date:			
Saturday Date:			
Sunday Date:			

Audio Activities for Session 1

Track 1: Beginner's Mind Activity

This practice will help you cultivate your "beginner's mind," which means to experience things as if for the first time. To practice in this way is to see and hear things with a newness, a freshness that appreciates and enjoys the experience in a deeper way. Many mindfulness teachers view beginner's mind practices as a key pathway to enjoying life.

Track 2: Body-Mindfulness Meditation

The body mindfulness exercise (also known as, and referred to interchangeably with, a *body scan*) is another classic mindfulness exercise. This involves bringing a careful, open, and accepting awareness to our body in the present moment. The purpose of this exercise is not relaxation – although that might happen for you – but the main purpose is simply awareness.

Track 3: You at Your Best and Strengths-Spotting

Think of a specific time, recently or a while back, when you were at your best. You were really feeling and acting at a high level and directly contributing to the positive experience. Perhaps you felt you were really engaged in what you were doing? Perhaps you felt like the experience you were part of was a very successful one? Most likely you felt like you were your authentic self, being who you are. It may have been a specific experience in a relationship, in a work or school environment, or while socializing. Reflect on this story. See if you can frame your experience with a beginning, middle, and end. **Be sure to consider the character strengths that you used in that experience.**

Take this a step further. One way is to quietly replay, in your mind, the positive experience and the strengths you use to contribute to it. You might also share the story with someone, brainstorm the character strengths that each of you observe in.

Practice Activities for Session 1

Practice Activity 1.1. Mindfulness With a Routine Activity

Ready to challenge your autopilot mind and make the most of your mindfulness?

This activity is a classic mindfulness practice that will help you engage your senses, build your mindfulness, and come to appreciate a part of your day that you likely take for granted most of the time. This practice involves acting with awareness, observing and describing your experience, and letting go of your mind's tendency to judge or react to the experience.

Steps

1. Choose one activity you do each day but do not feel "present" when doing it.
   - Perhaps when you brush your teeth, you are not paying attention to the feeling of the bristles against your teeth and gums, or when you wash your hair, you're not especially aware of the movement of your fingers and the scent of the shampoo.
   - Because going into autopilot is the default mode for the mind, you can select just about any activity you do each day: feeding your pet, getting the mail, dropping off your dry cleaning. You can choose the same activity each day for the whole week or try two or more routine activities throughout the week.
2. Bring greater mindfulness to the activity each time you do it, throughout the entire experience. This will help you slow down, direct your attention, and support what you're doing, one thing at a time.

Tips

- Use as many of your five senses as are relevant for the activity. Your senses will help you deepen your mindfulness.
- Remember to Catch AP-ASAP: Catch your autopilot mind, as soon as possible. The moment your mind criticizes the experience, gets bored, or wanders away by thinking of something else, gently bring it back to the activity.

Example

Routine activity: *Brushing my teeth*

Observations: *I noticed the rhythmic circular motions I make when brushing my upper teeth and the back-and-forth motions I make with my lower teeth. The hum of the electric toothbrush was constant and low, and the taste of the toothpaste was strong, with a spearmint flavor I could almost feel on the edge of my gums. I realize how quickly my mind wanders away from brushing to what I'm going to do next in my day.*

Mindfulness-Based Strengths Practice (MBSP)
Practice Worksheet 1.1: Mindfulness With a Routine Activity Tracking

Day 1

Routine activity: _____

Observations:

_____

_____

_____

_____

Day 2

Routine activity: _____

Observations:

_____

_____

_____

_____

Day 3

Routine activity: _____

Observations:

_____

_____

_____

_____

Day 4

Routine activity: _____

Observations:

_____

_____

_____

_____

Day 5

Routine activity: _____

Observations:

_____

_____

_____

_____

Day 6

Routine activity: _____

Observations:

_____

_____

_____

_____

Day 7

Routine activity: _____

Observations:

_____

_____

_____

_____

Reading Activities for Session 1

Mindfulness-Based Strengths Practice (MBSP)
Reading Activity 1.1: Overview of Mindfulness-Based Strengths Practice

Overview

Mindfulness-based strengths practice (MBSP) is an eight-session program that brings the science and practice of mindfulness and the science and practice of character strengths together. It includes discussions, meditations, strengths practices, lectures and input, and homework exercises. There are two general categories of integration:
1. **Strong mindfulness:** improving mindfulness practices by weaving in character strengths.
2. **Mindful strengths use:** improving character strength use by weaving in mindfulness.

Description

This 8-week program is about engaging more deeply with life. The crux is self-awareness and self-discovery. It combines two powerful and popular approaches that are being used in schools, clinics, universities, scientific labs, and businesses worldwide: *mindfulness* and *character strengths*. Emphasis is placed on exercises that are discussed and practiced each week. This course teaches the basics of mindfulness and of character strengths, and offers more advanced, practical ways to integrate the two. It presents a unique angle to living one's best life, rediscovering happiness, achieving goals, finding deeper meaning and life engagement, and coping with problems.

Practices

Participants practice mindful breathing, listening, speaking, eating, walking, mindfulness of problems, loving-gratitude meditation, and the mindful pause. In addition, participants practice strengths spotting, use of signature strengths, character strengths 360, strengths branding, strengths interview, valuing strengths in others, best possible self, strengths goal setting, strengths-activity mapping, strengths gathas, and many others.

Core sessions

Session 1: Mindfulness and Autopilot

The autopilot mind is pervasive; mindlessness, distractedness, and going through the motions of life are the default. At the same time, our mindful mind can be developed as a counterbalance and life enhancer. Insights and change opportunities start with the attention of our mindful mind.

Session 2: Your Character Strengths and Signature Strengths

Signature strengths are a subset of your 24 strengths of character. They are what is best in you. You can unlock your potential and find greater well-being, engagement, and meaning, by understanding, exploring, and using your signature strengths.

Session 3: Obstacles and Struggles Are Opportunities

The difficulties of life – conflicts, problems, and suffering – can become opportunities for mindfulness and character strengths. Learn how to take a strengths mindset with life challenges and with your mindfulness practice. This can lead to a wider appreciation for the little things in life. This mindset is also known as *strong mindfulness*.

Session 4: Strengthening Mindfulness in Everyday Life

You can strengthen mindfulness in your everyday life – your eating, listening, speaking, working, driving, and your walking. Character strengths provide a value-add to these experiences, offering new insights and a unique depth. Any action we take has the potential to be an action infused with the energy of mindfulness and the energy of character strengths.

Session 5: Your Relationship With Yourself and Others

Mindful attending can nourish two types of relationships: relationships with others and our relationship with ourselves. Our relationship with ourselves contributes to self-growth and can have an immediate impact on our connection with others. Using character strengths in this mindful way is known as *mindful strengths use*.

Session 6: Mindfulness of The Golden Mean

We regularly overuse and underuse our character strengths, and this can vary widely by the context and our own patterns. Mindfulness helps us discover optimal strengths use or a *golden mean* for our character strengths in any situation. This also presents powerful strengths-reframing opportunities for our problems and life challenges.

MBSP Retreat: Half-Day (this is noted here for those participating in an MBSP program; it is not described in this workbook)

Mindful living and character strengths apply not only to good meditation practice but also to daily conversation, eating, walking, sitting, reflecting, and the nuances therein (e.g., opening the refrigerator door, turning a doorknob, creating a smile). This day is therefore a practice day for these activities of living. It is also a practice day for both types of integration – strong mindfulness and mindful strengths use.

Session 7: Authenticity and Goodness

Consider your learnings and practices up to this point. Are you working toward becoming better at *being you* (authenticity), or are you focused on becoming a *better person* (goodness)? These overlapping approaches necessarily involve mindfulness and character strengths and can be woven into your aspirational (or goal-generating) approach to live your best life.

Session 8: Your Engagement With Life

Stick with those practices that have been working well and watch your mind's tendency to revert back to automatic habits that are deficit-based, unproductive, or ultimately self-defeating. Engage in an approach that fosters awareness and celebration of what is strongest in you and others.

Benefits

Research shows MBSP boosts many kinds of well-being such as happiness, personal growth, work satisfaction, and meaning in life. Studies show it improves close relationships and workplace productivity.

Purposes of MBSP

- Despite the many benefits of mindfulness, most people who start a mindfulness practice do not keep it up. Character strengths offer ways for individuals to better deal with obstacles and barriers that naturally emerge.
- The character strengths are a common language of positive qualities that can be noticed and enhanced by the energy of mindfulness.
- Mindfulness and character strengths are interdependent and can create a virtuous circle of mutual benefit.
- Mindfulness facilitates increased self-awareness and potential for change activation by bringing one's character strengths more clearly into view.
- This practice offers a path for individuals to use their best strengths, and be more attuned to a balanced expression that is sensitive to the situation and to potential overuse or underuse.

Session 2:
Your Character Strengths and Signature Strengths

Make the most of yourself, for that is all there is of you.

Ralph Waldo Emerson

A story to remember

Every day, I walk my dog in my neighborhood, which contains a short, wooded path. Rain, snow, extreme heat or cold, feelings of fatigue, sickness, or disinterest, I walk my dog. Even though my dog is only a few years old, I have done this habit hundreds of times. One summer day, toward the end of the wooded path, to my left, I saw a snake. I was quite surprised by this. The snake had no interest in me or my dog and merely lay coiled as I walked by. I've not seen a snake in the wood path since then. Although it was only one time out of hundreds, when I get to that spot on the path, my mind goes toward the left side and thinks of the snake. It is ingrained in my brain. It replays the snake being there – although harmless, it is a trigger. It is rooted deep in my consciousness, just like things that are dangerous or wrong or a worry or a deficit. I do not have a fear of snakes, nor do I have a lot of experience with them. Nevertheless, it is rooted in my mind.

This is surprising to me. Where is the wiring for the positive? There is much beauty, greenery, peacefulness, and nature to savor, to remember, and to also get "rooted" into my mind. There's the place where I saw a hummingbird fluttering near a tree or a squirrel that balanced itself along a fence. No, these are not as strong, and usually they are not remembered, certainly not remembered with the frequency of the one-time snake.

But, I have created an exception. There's a lotus pond at the midpoint of my journey. During a few months, there are more than one hundred, beautiful and striking flowers of white and pink, with green lillypads desperately competing to get close to the flowers. Sometimes they overwhelm the lotus covering them completely from the sun and at other times the lotus breaks free and stands beautiful and full on the surface of the water. Over my walks to the pond and around it, I have paused many times to observe, to be with the pond and its ecosystem. Sometimes I breathe with it, sometimes I study it, sometimes I write about it, sometimes I walk slowly around it. My mind, now, remembers the pond and the lotuses, and it looks for this "good." My mind has been trained to attend to it and to care for it. There are many people in my neighborhood who don't know there are lotus flowers in the pond, and who barely notice the pond is there. But, my mind is now wired for this beauty – wired to "see" and experience it – just as it is wired to see a snake that is not there.

Through positive intentionality, effort, and repetition, my mind has created a pattern or routine that is nourishing. It has ingrained something positive in my brain.

What Are Character Strengths?

We can become preoccupied with many things – pleasant and unpleasant. It's important to know we have some choice in the matter. One area of tremendous opportunity to become more attuned to, habitual with, and embedded in practice with is character strengths.

Character strengths are what's best in you. They are the core parts of your personality that reflect who you are. Their expression brings benefit to yourself, others, and the world. You might think of character strengths as an internal fountain. The water source is your body's center, and it flows within you and streams out to your relationships and the external world.

A set of 24 character strengths was discovered by scientists to exist across human beings of differing cultures, nations, and belief systems (see Box 1). These strengths – including gratitude, bravery, curiosity, kindness, honesty, and self-regulation – can be deployed to create a full life and to improve the lives of others. These strengths are different from other types of assets we possess, such as talents (abilities and things we do well, such as sports or music), skills (proficiencies we develop, such as typing or public speaking), interests (passions we have, such as hobbies or making art), and external resources (our family and community supports).

At the end of this chapter (Practice Activity 2.3), you'll find an example of a Character Strengths Fluency Builder. This offers a different view of "the language of character strengths" from Box 1. This example provides one way for you to personalize your understanding of character strengths and help you to "learn the language" – to become fluent with the words, their meanings, how they connect with your behavior, etc.

Why Do Character Strengths Matter?

Character strengths are the fuel that makes us soar both personally and professionally, in our home life and our work life. The last decade has seen an explosion of research on character strengths that reveals a multitude of

---

Box 1. VIA Classification of six virtues and 24 character strengths

Virtue of Wisdom: strengths that help you gather and use knowledge
- Creativity: being original; seeing/doing things in new ways
- Curiosity: exploring; seeking novelty; open to experiences
- Judgment: critical thinking; rational-minded; thinking things through
- Love of learning: mastering new skills & topics; building knowledge
- Perspective: providing wise counsel; taking a big picture view

Virtue of Courage: strengths that help you exercise your will and face adversity
- Bravery: facing fears, threats, or challenges; speaking up for what's right
- Perseverance: persisting; finishing what is started; overcoming obstacles
- Honesty: telling the truth; being authentic; being sincerity
- Zest: being energetic; enthusiastic; doing things wholeheartedly

Virtue of Humanity: strengths that help you in one-on-one relationships
- Love: being genuine; showing warmth; valuing close relationships
- Kindness: being generous; caring; compassionate; nice and friendly
- Social intelligence: being aware of feelings & motives of self/others; acting accordingly

Virtue of Justice: strengths that help you in community or group-based situations
- Teamwork: being loyal; contributing to group efforts
- Fairness: acting justly; not letting feelings bias decisions
- Leadership: organizing a group to get things done; positively guiding others

Temperance: strengths that help you manage habits and protect against excess
- Forgiveness: being merciful; accepting others' shortcomings; letting go of hurts
- Humility: being modest; placing attention on others; not bragging
- Prudence: being careful about choices; cautious; not taking undue risks
- Self-regulation: being self-controlled; disciplined; manages impulses & emotions

Transcendence: strengths that help you connect to the larger universe and provide meaning
- Appreciation of beauty/excellence: experiencing awe, wonder, admiration, elevation
- Gratitude: being thankful for the good in life; sharing thanks; feeling blessed
- Hope: being optimistic; positive; future-minded; expecting the best
- Humor: being playful, seeing the lighter side, bringing smiles to others
- Spirituality: searching for meaning; feeling purpose in life; connecting with the sacred

benefits from nurturing them, ranging from greater flourishing, resilience, engagement, meaning, relationship intimacy and commitment, to less stress. In the workplace, employees who apply character strengths are more productive; in school settings, children are happier and achieve more. And benefits have been found in other domains such as health, parenting, and counseling, as well.

We feel happier and more energized when we use our strengths. When we express our strengths to others (such as forgiveness, fairness, and love), it helps those we care about and improves our relationships with them. Further, when we validate and appreciate others' strengths, we feel good and contribute to their well-being. Ultimately, this creates ripples of positivity running throughout our relationships and networks as we contribute to the greater good.

Do's and don'ts of reviewing your VIA Survey results

DO look at all 24 character strengths. All of your strengths matter.

DO give most attention to understanding and appreciating your highest strengths.

DO reflect on how you use your highest strengths each day. Your strength behaviors matter.

DON'T compare your strength rankings to others. Compare *you to you*, not *you to others.*

DON'T hyperfocus on your lowest character strengths. These are not weaknesses or deficits; they are lesser strengths.

DON'T deny or reject your highest strengths. Remember, you answered the questions. These capture the "real you" in some ways.

Your Character Strengths Profile

There is one main test that is free, scientifically valid, and measures the many character strengths that make up what is best in you: the VIA Survey (https://www.viacharacter.org/; also called the VIA Inventory of Strengths; see also Reading Activity 2.1, for a fact sheet about the VIA Institute that created the test). Take the test now, in which you will answer questions about your curiosity, fairness, teamwork, self-regulation, hope, bravery, and creativity. The test is designed to help you identify your best strengths of character – the most positive parts of who you are. After you complete the test (it takes about 10 minutes), you will receive immediate results of your rank order of character strengths from highest strength to lowest strength.

Exploring Your Results

There are many ways you can view your survey results. You can concentrate on your highest strengths (also called your *signature strengths*), your lowest strengths, the strengths that surprise you the most, or the strengths that disappointed you (because you had expected or hoped for other strengths to be high in your profile). You can look to strengths you use on autopilot and those you use at times of distress. You can work to improve any of them.

Here are a few questions to help you explore your results further. As you do so, know that any kind of reaction to them is OK – there is no right or wrong way to feel. Considering that there are 24 strengths that each carry their own definition and uses, you might benefit from reading up on some of them for more clarity as you assess your results. Go to https://www.viacharacter.org/ to learn, watch, and read more on any of the 24 character strengths.

? What strikes you the most about your rank-order profile? As you review your profile, be mindful of your feelings and reactions.

_____

_____

_____

_____

? What do you feel happy and excited about? What triggers joy and intrigue in you from your results?

_____

_____

_____

_____

? Was there anything disappointing or even upsetting in your results? Did you find yourself strongly disagreeing with something? Be honest with yourself as you explore your reaction here.

_____

_____

_____

_____

? Next, describe a recent positive experience you had from any area of your life. Include what went well in the situation and how you contributed to that.

_____

_____

_____

_____

Now go back over what you just wrote in the last question and circle any of the 24 character strengths that you recognize in this experience, either the literal words themselves or the parts of your experience that reflect one of the strengths. For example, if you wrote about helping a friend with a problem, that's kindness; if you thought of a new way to solve a problem, that's creativity; if you said the word "interested" then that likely reflects some curiosity.

Congratulations! With this last action, you've begun the important practice of *strengths-spotting*. When you engage in strengths-spotting, you spot the character strengths in the actions of others and in yourself. You can look to the past, or you can notice strengths as they are happening in the present moment. As you grow in your mindful awareness, you'll be able to more quickly notice the positive qualities in yourself and others with greater ease and joy.

 YOUR MINDFUL PAUSE

Pause for a moment. Close your eyes and breathe for 15 seconds. Focus only on your in-breath and your out-breath.

Ask yourself: *Which of my character strengths might I bring forth right now?*

Take action with the character strength that rises strongest within you. This might be an action in your thinking, your words, or your actions – right now, or in your near future.

Mindful Recognition and Appreciation of Your Signature Strengths

All 24 character strengths in your profile are important. Your highest, middle, and lower strengths – they all matter, and you use them all at different times. It is your highest strengths, your unique signature strengths, that probably matter the most, because these are the strengths that get at the real you – who you are when you are being authentic with others. Although no set of words can perfectly capture the full complexity of who you are, it is likely your signature strengths capture a good portion of your essence and what others appreciate about you.

It's easy to take our signature strengths for granted, to assume we already know enough about them. In fact, research indicates that most people believe they know their strengths already. The problem is, they're wrong. When it comes to our strengths, there's a whole lot we're *unaware* of. This is referred to as *strengths blindness*. There are many ways we neglect, avoid, or overlook our strengths. Consider these individuals who were asked the simple question, "What are your strengths?"

- Jamie heard the question and looked down at his shoes. "I don't know. That's not something I've given much thought to," he said.
- Raquel, who was typically a very talkative person, became quiet, and then shared, "I try not to talk about that."
- Blaine explained, "I like to watch documentary movies. I collect stamps, and I go out on weekends with friends." When pushed to share what drives these interest areas, he did not have much to add.
- Allala pointed out a couple of her character strengths: "I learned I'm high in self-regulation and fairness." When asked to share an example of how she has used the strengths, she could not come up with any.

These are all examples of different kinds of character strength blindness. Each person seems unable to connect with the question or with their best qualities. We all have some level of strengths blindness; no one is perfectly self-aware. But there is action you can take. There are an abundant number of ways you can deepen your understanding and expand upon your character strengths and your highest, signature strengths. This Workbook will be your guide.

Your next step can be to take a look at each of your top five strengths. Look for the good in each. See how each is an important part of you. As you focus on two questions about each strength – how it connects with your identity (who you are in this world) and why it means something to you – you'll be participating in the process of confirming, endorsing, and appreciating your signature strengths.

Your #1 character strength: _____

? What do you like about this strength in you? _____

_____

_____

_____

_____

_____

_____

? How does this strength bring benefit to you or to others when you use it?

_____

_____

_____

_____

_____

_____

? What is one of your favorite ways that you use this strength?

_____

_____

_____

_____

_____

_____

Your #2 character strength: _____

? What do you like about this strength in you? _____

_____

_____

_____

_____

_____

? How does this strength bring benefit to you or to others when you use it?

_____

_____

_____

_____

_____

? What is one of your favorite ways that you use this strength?

_____

_____

_____

_____

_____

Your #3 character strength: _____

(?) What do you like about this strength in you? _____

_____

_____

_____

_____

_____

(?) How does this strength bring benefit to you or to others when you use it?

_____

_____

_____

_____

_____

(?) What is one of your favorite ways that you use this strength?

_____

_____

_____

_____

_____

Your #4 character strength: _____

? What do you like about this strength in you? _____

_____

_____

_____

_____

_____

_____

? How does this strength bring benefit to you or to others when you use it?

_____

_____

_____

_____

_____

_____

? What is one of your favorite ways that you use this strength?

_____

_____

_____

_____

_____

_____

Your #5 character strength: _____

? What do you like about this strength in you? _____

_____

_____

_____

_____

_____

? How does this strength bring benefit to you or to others when you use it?

_____

_____

_____

_____

_____

_____

? What is one of your favorite ways that you use this strength?

_____

_____

_____

_____

_____

_____

The exploration you have now completed will help you to better understand your best strengths and ways you use them. But, appreciation of your strengths goes beyond acknowledgment of the benefits of each one. A true, mindful appreciation for your best qualities goes deep. It's honest and humble to see, appreciate, and express your strengths.

How deeply do you appreciate your best qualities? How would you be impacted if they were gone?

To really take hold of this mindful appreciation, let's engage in a two-part experiment.

Focus on your #1 character strength in your profile or whichever strength in your top five feels most like "the real you." Picture this strength and how you have used it in so many ways in you life. Consider how it has helped you in your relationships, with your health, in managing stress, and in your achievements. It has helped you in more ways than you can count. Take time to really appreciate this core quality that has been existing in you for so many years. Pause in your reading right now to appreciate how much this strength has helped you.

? Write your appreciative thoughts here:

_____

_____

_____

_____

_____

_____

_____

_____

_____

_____

_____

_____

_____

_____

_____

Now for the second part. Sometimes we best learn about the value of something by seeing life without it. Imagine that you are not able to use the strength you selected, for 1 month. For the next month, you cannot bring forth this strength in any way. Not in your actions, your words, your relationships, or your work. Not even in your thinking and feeling. What would that be like? How would it feel to not have that core quality for one month? Find the strength you selected in Table 1. Read that example. Then, close your eyes and reflect on what your life would be like without that strength. Allow yourself to get a "felt sense" in your body and feelings around not having the strength.

Table 1.   Mental subtraction of a signature strength: Life without your best quality

Character strength being omitted	Imagine your life without this strength for the next month. Examples:
Creativity	You cannot create anything new – blogging, e-mails, social media, photographs, drawings, etc. You cannot come up with new ways to solve any of your problems. You cannot brainstorm or consider any new ideas at work, school, or home. You pursue life without a sense of freshness.
Curiosity	You cannot pursue new activities, explore or investigate anything, ask anyone any questions, try new foods, go anywhere new in your city, search on the Internet or your phone, or pursue anything novel or different for the next month. You pursue life without exploration.
Judgment	You cannot look at the details of anything. You cannot offer a rational or logical response in your conversation. You cannot analyze anything in your work or life. You cannot have an open mind to ideas, opinions, or projects. You pursue life without analysis.
Love of learning	You cannot pursue learning of any kind. You cannot learn from your mistakes, learn about new topics or subject matters, or take part in in any class, course, degree, certification, or area of development. You cannot learn about what's going on in the world or in the lives of others. You pursue life without new knowledge.
Perspective	You cannot give advice or insights to others or to yourself. You cannot see *the bigger picture,* the mission, or the underlying purpose or intention of anything in your work or school. You cannot draw any connections between your daily actions and your goals. You pursue life without vision.
Bravery	You cannot challenge yourself with any project or task. You cannot move out of your comfort zone in your social life and relationships. You cannot face or take action with any of your fears, anxieties, or stressors. You cannot speak to what's on your mind, disagree with anyone, or share a less popular opinion. You pursue life without courage.
Perseverance	You cannot finish anything that you start. This includes work projects, daily routines, and conversations. You cannot work hard or make an effort with any action you take in life. You cannot overcome obstacles or challenges that come up as you pursue a goal. You pursue life without a will (drive).
Honesty	You cannot tell the truth to anyone. You cannot give any answers or responses, directly or indirectly, to people's questions. You cannot be authentic and true to who you are in any of your relationships. You cannot be consistent in your actions at work, home, and social life. You pursue life without integrity.

Table 1.   Continued

Character strength being omitted	Imagine your life without this strength for the next month. Examples:
Zest	You cannot show enthusiasm in your conversations, nor can you feel excited about anything that happens in your life. You cannot take any action except those that are half-hearted or halfway. You cannot feel a sense of vigor or be active in any way in your lifestyle. You pursue life without energy.
Love	You cannot be warm to people in your life. You cannot be an attentive listener in conversation. You must evaporate any sense of genuineness in your life. You cannot value or appreciate your close relationships. You cannot hug, kiss, or touch anyone in a loving way. You pursue life without closeness.
Kindness	You cannot help other people. This means you cannot be caring, generous, or nice to anyone. You cannot show compassion and understanding to those in need or to those you connect with. You cannot do any small, thoughtful acts, nor can you offer words of support to anyone. You also cannot be caring to yourself. You pursue life without goodness.
Social intelligence	You cannot be aware of your feelings or the feelings of others in any situation and you cannot express any feelings to others. You cannot get a general sense for a situation or a *read* on what is happening in a social environment. You cannot look at any facial expressions, body language, or notice any voice tone, intensity, or emotionality in yourself or others. You pursue life without connection.
Teamwork	You cannot contribute in a positive way to a team you are on. This means you cannot offer support, loyalty, or helpful interactions in your work team, sport team, volunteer or community group, spiritual community, social groups, or your family, nor can you view your intimate relationship as a *team*. You cannot do your share of the work. You cannot meaningfully contribute to your organization or school by helping it to reach its vision or make any positive impact in the larger community. You pursue life without collaboration.
Fairness	You let your personal feelings bias every decision you make. You never give people a fair chance or an equal opportunity. You cannot pursue any issues of justice, equity, or diversity, nor can you engage in any inclusion practices. You cannot do what is morally right in any situation. You pursue life without justice.
Leadership	You cannot positively influence others. You cannot organize any groups or activities involving others. You cannot share a vision for people to follow. You cannot use your character strengths to lead others forward or to improvement. You pursue life without inspiration.
Forgiveness	You cannot give anyone a second chance after they've made a mistake. You cannot show mercy to people, animals, trees, or other life forms. You cannot let go of little things such as daily frustrations, stressors, or minor irritations; everything bothers you and consumes you. You pursue life without acceptance.
Humility	You cannot focus on others in a positive way. You cannot think of yourself in a balanced way, only arrogance and ego-driven selfishness. You do not see any limitations, weaknesses, or struggles within yourself. You walk through life thinking and feeling like you are better than everyone at everything. You pursue life without groundedness.
Prudence	You cannot be careful about any choice you make. You cannot set short-term or long-term goals for your day, week, or year. You cannot think before you speak. You cannot think before you act at work or home. You cannot be respectful of others. You cannot be on time nor conscientious about anything. You pursue life without pausing.

Table 1.   Continued

Character strength being omitted	Imagine your life without this strength for the next month. Examples:
Self-regulation	You cannot be self-disciplined with your health, including eating, drinking, activity level, sleep activities, or self-care. You cannot manage your impulses, your vices, or your inner drives. You cannot control your emotions, whether that be controlling your anger, sadness, or anxiety. You pursue life without balance.
Appreciation of beauty	You cannot feel the emotions of wonder, awe, or admiration, even a little. This means you walk through life as if you have blinders on, especially when you are in nature, in new cities, the countryside, or near oceans or lakes, when you are observing skillful people (e.g., athletes, musicians), or when people are connecting with one another. You cannot feel inspired or uplifted when someone does something kind, fair, creative, or brave. You pursue life without your senses.
Gratitude	You cannot express thankfulness to anyone regardless of what they do, say, or give to you. You cannot even feel any appreciation or sense of good will for the positives in your life or the care by others. You feel no connection or sense of feeling blessed for anything. You pursue life without any appreciation for it.
Hope	You cannot be optimistic or positive about anything. You cannot ever find the silver lining in any challenge or stressor. You cannot look or plan for the future. You cannot feel confident about any goals or intentions you have for your work or life. You pursue life without intention.
Humor	You cannot smile or laugh, or make others laugh. You cannot be playful and cheerful. You cannot tell jokes, funny stories, or see the lighter side of things. You cannot pursue pleasure in your life. You pursue life without joy.
Spirituality	You cannot feel or sense any connection outside of yourself. You cannot express virtues or goodness or live a virtuous life. You cannot engage in any spiritual seeking or spiritual practices, rituals, community connecting, or sacred readings. You cannot have any beliefs relating to the universe, death, or purpose in life. You pursue life without meaning.

?   After a few minutes, write down, using a few words or phrases, what it felt like to *not* have the strength:

_____

_____

_____

_____

_____

? What does this experience tell you about this signature strength of yours?

_____

_____

_____

_____

_____

_____

Research studies have shown that this activity, referred to by scientists as *mental subtraction,* is a successful strategy to boost your well-being. It deepens your appreciation of your strengths. Oftentimes, we don't realize how meaningful and important something is to us until it is gone.

Consider repeating this activity for each of your signature strengths. Give special attention to the signature strengths that you are most blind to or mindless about.

Signature Strengths Use

You've now done some exploring and appreciating of your signature strengths. Now it's time to put your results into action by learning how to *use* your strengths.

Research shows that when people expand upon their highest strengths, they can improve their happiness and flourishing and lessen their depression. In some studies, individuals who make a conscious effort to expand their signature strengths experience the benefits of this effort for 6 months. So the overall goal is to figure out new ways to use your signature strengths each day. You might apply your strength to your actions (e.g., doing something kind), your thoughts (e.g., using prudent thinking to plan an activity for the weekend), your feelings (e.g., noticing feelings of hope or zest in a situation), or your interactions with others (expressing gratefulness to someone). Box 2 shows examples for how you might use any of your character strengths.

Box 2. Twenty-four examples of character strengths use

Use your creativity: Think of one of your problems and three possible solutions to it. Summarize these solutions in a way that is not typical for you, such as in a drawing, in a reflective meditation, or in a conversation.

Use your curiosity: Try a new food for the first time, preferably from a culture different from your own.

Use your judgment/critical thinking: Watch a political program from the opposite point of view of your own and keep an open mind.

Use your love of learning: Do an online search of your favorite subject matter and surprise yourself by learning something new about it.

Use your perspective: For one of your interactions today: First, listen closely and consider what you have heard; then, share your ideas and thoughts.

Use your bravery: Consider one of your personal fears. Take one small, healthy action toward facing it today.

Use your perseverance: Overcome the obstacles and complete a small project that you have been putting off.

Use your honesty: Contact a family member or friend to whom you have told a partial truth and give them the complete details.

Use your zest: Exert your energy in a unique way – jump on a bed, run in place, practice yoga or body stretching, or chase around a child or pet.

Use your love: Tell someone about a strength you saw them use and how much you value them as a person for their strengths.

Use your kindness: Stop by a hospital or nursing home and offer to visit someone who is lonely , or be particularly thoughtful and caring toward the person working the front desk or the janitor outside.

Use your social intelligence: Start up a conversation with someone whom you normally would not say much more to than typical pleasantries.

Use your teamwork: Spot and express appreciation for the strengths shown by one or two of your team members.

Use your fairness: Include someone in a conversation who is typically excluded from groups or is a newcomer.

Use your leadership: Discuss with someone who reports to you about how they can align their top character strength more in their work.

Use your forgiveness: Consider a minor offense someone committed or a daily irritant, and let it go – release it from your feelings and thoughts.

Use your humility: Ask someone you trust to give you feedback on your struggles and growth areas.

Use your prudence: Before you make a decision that is typically very easy, take one full minute to think about it before you take action.

Use your self-regulation: The next time you feel irritated or nervous today, pause and breathe with the experience for a count of 5 breathes.

Use your appreciation of beauty and excellence: Go outside and stand still in a beautiful environment for 10 minutes.

Use your gratitude: Tell someone "thanks" who deserves it and is typically not recognized.

Use your hope: Consider a problem or struggle you are having. Write down two optimistic, realistic thoughts that bring comfort.

Use your humor: Do something spontaneous and playful around another person (e.g., saying something silly, contorting your body in a weird way, or telling a funny story or joke).

Use your spirituality: Contemplate the *sacredness* of this present moment. Allow yourself to find meaning in the moment.

Which of these strategies stands out most for you? Look at the examples of your signature strengths first. Then, look to other character strengths you might focus on. Write down the two strategies you're most interested in trying out this week.

_____

_____

_____

_____

_____

_____

_____

_____

_____

_____

_____

_____

_____

_____

_____

_____

_____

_____

_____

_____

_____

_____

One of the activities at the end of this chapter will guide you to expand your practice using your signature strengths in new ways this week. Use the examples in Box 2 to help you start taking action today.

 DID YOU KNOW?

Across many studies around the globe, 5 character strengths have repeatedly emerged as most connected with happiness. These are zest, hope, love, gratitude, and curiosity (Gander et al., 2013).

You have now learned two ways you can use your strengths to create greater happiness:
1. Use your signature strengths in new ways.
2. Use one of the five happiness strengths more deliberately in your life.

Essential Tips for Developing Your Strengths Practice

1. **Know your 24.** To make the most of your strengths practice, you'll want to become fluent in the *common language* of character strengths. Keep a list of the 24 strengths in a highly visible place: on your fridge, in your smartphone, by your computer, on your nightstand. You can print out Reading Activity 2.2 or create your own list. Review it often. Get to know what is meant by each strength – the synonyms for each, the dimensions of each, and what they look like in action.

2. **Keep character strengths on the tip of your tongue, not in the back of your mind.** Keep strengths in "action mode" at the forefront of your mind; otherwise, you'll forget them. Talk about them in both planned and spontaneous ways. Be both casual and formal, general and specific. The more you talk about them, the more they will become part of your thought processes and behaviors. This will help you develop *strengths mindfulness,* a solid and embodied consciousness about your character strengths each day.

3. **Anchor your strengths with daily routines.** In Session 1, you brought mindfulness to a routine activity each day. You can also anchor one character strength to a routine activity each day. For example, you might start by anchoring fairness to talking with your spouse or partner after work. As such, the conversation becomes your daily cue – to be fair in the conversation itself, in the conflicts that come up, in the listening-to-

speaking ratio, and so on. Over time, fairness will become a deeply entrenched part of that activity. Other examples include anchoring prudence to making meals, kindness to driving on the expressway, gratitude to social media correspondence, and curiosity to writing e-mails. Choose any strength to link with a given activity, then stick with that strength anchor for that particular daily activity for a week. At the end of each day, ask yourself, *How did I use my strengths anchor today?*

Let's turn to some practices you can use throughout the week to build your character strengths. Just as the activities at the end of Session 1 laid the groundwork for your mindfulness practice, here you'll take the same approach with your character strengths practice. You are already off to a great start with the Mindfulness of a Routine Activity and your Body-Mindfulness Practice, so keep those going strong each day! In addition, listen to the short new meditation (Character Strengths Breathing Space) and practice Using Your Signature Strengths in New Ways each day. After you do these fun and meaningful activities for about one week, you'll be ready for Session 3.

Your MBSP Toolbox
Session 2: Character Strengths and Signature Strengths

Key Insights

- There are 24 universal character strengths you have that are part of your core identity. They help you to build well-being while also managing adversity in life. All 24 of these strengths matter.

- You have bravery, perseverance, hope, gratitude, curiosity, creativity, kindness, leadership, humility, and forgiveness within you. You can discover your unique character strengths profile (your rank-order of strengths from 1 to 24) by taking the free VIA Survey at www.viacharacter.org.

- Character strengths blindness is pervasive. You can counter this by taking time to be mindful of your top strengths and appreciate each one, in turn.

From the Science

- Multiple scientific studies have shown that using one of your signature strengths in a new way each day can boost happiness and flourishing and decrease depression for as long as six months (Gander et al., 2013).

For Your Exploration

- What strikes you most as you look at your full rank-order of strengths in your VIA Survey results (your character strengths profile)?

- What do you like about your highest strengths? How do each of your top strengths bring benefit to you?

Pearl of Wisdom

- Improve any of the 24 character strengths by anchoring it to a daily routine so you'll remember it and deepen in. Pair the strengths use with a meal, a snack, a daily conversation, when you make coffee, when you log into your computer, or other regular actions you take.

Expand Your Toolbox

- Sit with one of your signature strengths and spend time appreciating the value of it for your life.

- Mentally subtract one of your signature strengths. What would it feel like to not have the strength in your actions, words, feelings, or thoughts?

- Practice the Character Strengths Breathing Space (Audio Track 4). This practice helps you develop your strengths of curiosity, self-regulation, and perspective, as well as your mindful attention.

- Use one of your signature strengths in a new way each day (Practice Activity 2.1).

Mindfulness-Based Strengths Practice (MBSP)
Activities and Tracking Sheet: Session 2

Suggested Activities for This Week

- Body-Mindfulness Meditation (Audio Track 2). Practice ×1/day.
- Character Strengths Breathing Space exercise (Audio Track 4).
- Use one of your signature strengths in a new way each day (see Practice Activity 2.1 and Practice Worksheet 2.1).
- Complete Practice Activity 2.2 to take a deeper look at your VIA Survey results..
- Work on your Character Strengths Fluency Builder (Practice Activity 2.3).
- Track your experiences in this sheet or in your journal.
- **Bonus**: Select a current book you are reading, a TV show you watch, or recent movie or play you saw and write about the strengths you spot in the main character(s).

Day & date	Type of practice & time length	Strengths used	Observations & comments
Monday Date:			
Tuesday Date:			
Wednesday Date:			
Thursday Date:			
Friday Date:			
Saturday Date:			
Sunday Date:			

Audio Activities for Session 2

Track 2: Body-Mindfulness Meditation

Continue your practice with this meditation.

Track 4: Character Strengths Breathing Space Meditation

The Character Strengths Breathing Space exercise is a way to "frame in" the beginning and end of sessions. This is a 3-minute meditation that has three steps, each about 1 minute long. It has been adapted from mindfulness-based cognitive therapy (Segal et al., 2002) in a way that keeps mindfulness as the central element but it also highlights the character strengths involved in mindfulness. The intention is zo provide a brief "space" to help you be aware in the present moment and to connect with your breath while using chracter strengths.

Practice Activities for Session 2

Practice Activity 2.1. Use Your Signature Strengths in New Ways

The identification and use of signature strengths – those parts that are the best of you – is a classic activity in positive psychology. It has been shown to be successful across cultures and populations, in boosting well-being and life satisfaction, as well as in lowering depression. To bring forth your signature strengths in a balanced way is to express your authentic self.

Steps

1. As you review your rank-ordered results on the VIA Survey, select one of your top five strengths to focus on this week.
2. Reflect on the many ways you have used this signature strength throughout your life. Consider how your thinking is driven by this strength, locate where you feel this strength in your body, and identify how you act from this strength, in ways both large and small, when you're alone and when you're with others.
3. Use this strength in one new way each day. As you do so, you'll be expanding the ways in which you express yourself. Use Practice Worksheet 2.1 to write down your observations.

Mindfulness-Based Strengths Practice (MBSP)
Practice Worksheet 2.1: Use Your Signature Strengths in New Ways Tracking Sheet

My signature strength: _____

Day 1

New way:

_____

_____

_____

How I felt:

_____

_____

_____

Day 2

New way:

_____

_____

_____

_____

How I felt:

_____

_____

_____

_____

Day 3

New way:

_____

_____

_____

_____

How I felt:

_____

_____

_____

_____

Day 4

New way:

_____

_____

_____

_____

How I felt:

_____

_____

_____

_____

Day 5

New way:

_____

_____

_____

How I felt:

_____

_____

_____

Day 6

New way:

_____

_____

_____

How I felt:

_____

_____

_____

Day 7

New way:

_____

_____

_____

How I felt:

_____

_____

_____

Practice Activity 2.2: Exploring Strengths

Take the VIA Survey online (https://www.viacharacter.org/) and review your resulting list of strengths from 1 to 24. Explore your reaction to these results. **Read the following questions and circle those that stand out to you.** It might be helpful to ask "Why?" or "How?" after many of the questions:

- Do the top strengths seem like the "real you" – the core of who you are?
- When you use your top strengths, does it feel authentic?
- What is your gut reaction to the results?
- What surprises you most about the results?
- Which strengths seem to make you feel happy when you use them?
- Which strengths are you most interested in learning more about?
- What are your signature strengths? In other words, which strengths are most authentically you, come natural to you, and give you energy when you practice them?
- Which of your signature strengths are you least aware of (not tuned into when you are using them)?
- Which strengths do you feel a sense of yearning, in which you would like to use them more?
- When you think about a time when you were functioning at your best, which strengths did you use? Write this out as a story. Share it with someone.
- Which strengths give you a sense of excitement and enthusiasm as you think about using them? In other words, which strengths make you feel happy?
- When you think of a time when you were anxious, depressed, or highly stressed, which strengths did you use to move forward?
- Consider your past or current mentors (or personal role models, living or dead). What strengths did they embody? How did they express them? What strengths did they see in you?
- Which of the higher strengths are you most interested in building upon and expanding?
- Which of your lower strengths are you interested in building up?
- Which strengths are best for you to use in your family and relationship life, in your work life, and in your social life? Note that in each domain the combination of strengths you use might be very different.
- Which strengths might you use to reach your goals and/or to create a better future for yourself?
- Which strengths do you practice regularly? And which strengths just seem to come naturally where you do not even think about them until you are already using them?
- Which strength might might you ask a friend or family member for encouragement and support as you attempt to bring greater mindfulness to it?

Practice Activity 2.3: Character Strengths Fluency Builder

Creating a Character Strengths Fluency Builder offers a creative way of learning the language of character strengths. The aim of this activity is to create a visual mind map, diagram, flowchart or mnemonic that will help you connect, learn, and remember the language of character strengths. Practice Worksheet 2.3 provides an example of how you could map out the strengths you'd like to use for the goal of "family peace" or "workplace leadership." You can really let loose with your imagination and use whatever materials are handy – color pens or pencils, images cut from magazines, stickers.

Steps

- Draw a circle in the center of your page and inside, write your aspiration for life, something important for your life journey, or a particular goal. This can be a couple of words or a phrase such as "meaning," "connection," "flourishing," "family peace," "thriving and resilience," etc.
- Write down the six virtues of the VIA Classification (i.e., wisdom, courage, etc.), with arrows pointing to the center.
- Write in the 24 character strengths, each near the virtue category they nest under.
- Personalize this by calling out your signature strengths with a circle, star, symbol, or color.
- You can further personalize this by calling out strengths that help you be more resilient, strengths that make you feel happiest when you use them, strengths that help you connect with others, strengths that help you feel inner peace, strengths you want to improve upon, and strengths that help you rise to the occasion and which you can use when you really need them (also called phasic strengths).
- If there are strengths you want to better understand, you might add the dimensions, definitions, or other words near them as reminders. For example, for judgment, a person might write – critical thinking, open-minded, rationality, logic, analysis, 360 degrees of details. For kindness, someone might write the dimensions of this strengths – compassionate, generous, caring, altruistic, nice and friendly.

Additional tips:

- Along the way, infuse in color, symbols, connections, pictures, concepts, additional personalizations and comments, quotations, etc.
- If you have taken a mindfulness test such as the Five Facet Mindfulness Questionnaire, write in your highest mindfulness skills (or one you want to work on). This can serve as a helpful short language for mindfulness, just as we have the language for character strengths. The full list is observing, describing, acting with awareness, nonjudging, and nonreacting.
- Keep your Character Strengths Fluency Builder nearby as you engage in MBSP sessions and practices. In addition, be sure to add more details to it as you gain insights.

Mindfulness-Based Strengths Practice (MBSP)
Practice Worksheet 2.2: Character Strengths Fluency Builder Example

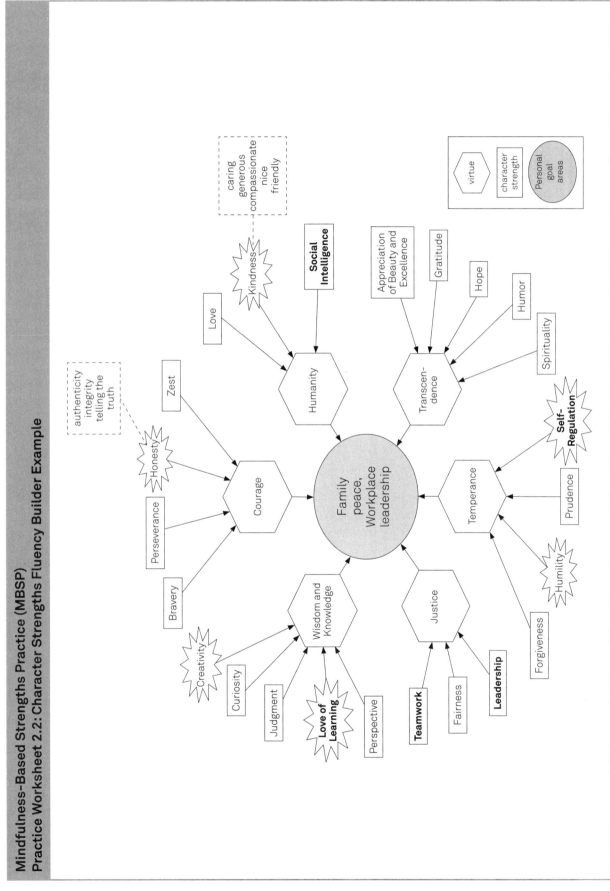

Note. This is one example. Each person should "create their own" in a way that engages their creativity and helps enhance their understanding of this "common language of strengths." No two fluency builders are the same.

〰️ = Character strengths I can use to work towards my goals; ----- = Descriptions of certain strengths; bold = My signature strengths

Reading Activities for Session 2

Mindfulness-Based Strengths Practice (MBSP)
Reading Activity 2.1: VIA Fact Sheet

VIA Institute

- The VIA Institute on Character (once called the Values in Action Institute) was created in 2000 by Dr. Neal Mayerson, in collaboration with Dr. Martin Seligman, founder of positive psychology.
- The mission of the VIA Institute is to advance the science and practice of character strengths.
- The VIA Institute on Character is a global, nonprofit organization located in Cincinnati, Ohio.
- Dr. Ryan Niemiec, the author of this book and creator of mindfulness-based strengths practice (MBSP) and the MBSP Certification, has worked at VIA since 2009. He is chief science and education officer there.

VIA Classification

- The VIA Classification is the result of a 3-year project reviewing the best thinking on virtue and positive human qualities in philosophy, virtue ethics, moral education, psychology, and theology, over the past 2,600 years (e.g., from the works of Aristotle and Benjamin Franklin, to King Charlemagne and the tenets of the major world religions).
- This project involved cross-cultural interviews with remote cultures, surveys across countries and all continents (except Antarctica), extensive historical review, and analysis using specific strength criteria.
- The work was conducted under the auspices of the VIA Institute, Dr. Seligman, 55 scientists and scholars, and directed by professor–researcher Dr. Chris Peterson.
- Six core themes emerged – wisdom, courage, humanity, justice, temperance, and transcendence – found across religions, cultures, nations, and belief systems.
- Applying various criteria, these *virtues* were subdivided into 24 universal character strengths that represent the pathways to the virtues.
- This work is discussed at length in the scholarly text by Peterson and Seligman, *Character Strengths and Virtues: A Handbook and Classification* (Peterson & Seligman, 2004), published by Oxford University Press and the American Psychological Association.

VIA Surveys (www.viacharacter.org)

- The VIA Survey (i.e., VIA Inventory of Strengths; VIA-IS; at https://www.viacharacter.org/) measures the 24 character strengths.
- The VIA Survey has been taken by over 27 million people (as of 2022) across every country around the globe and translated into nearly 50 languages. It gives the user immediate feedback on their top strengths of character. It is the only character strengths survey in the world that is free, online, and psychometrically valid.
- It has been found to have good, acceptable levels of reliability and validity.
- Results moderately correlate with reports by the respondent's friends and family.
- The VIA Youth Survey (i.e., VIA Inventory of Strengths for Youth) is a validated measure of the 24 character strengths in youths between the ages of 8 and 17 years. Youths receive free results.
- There are more than 20 additional validated measures of character strengths, freely available to researchers to study and collect data. These includes several brief measures; measures of virtues, signature strengths, and partner relationship strengths; direct measures of virtues; and several measures in development.

Professionals

Navigate the www.viacharacter.org site with the *tabs that are shown in bold* below:
- **Reports:** After anyone takes the VIA Survey, they are given immediate, free results for their character strengths profile. Many people want more details, practices, and graphs that are personalized to them, and therefore purchase an additional report. There are many to choose from on the Reports tab.
- **Courses:** Take MBSP live and virtually. Earn MBSP Certification. Take an on-demand course on character strengths. Explore various choices at the Courses tab.
- **Professionals:** Manage client, student, or employee VIA Survey results; get your own URL for clients; and many more resources.
- **Topics:** Explore character strengths with article and video resources for various topic areas such as mindfulness, happiness, stress, career building, relationships, and meaning in life.

Character

- **Definition:** Character strengths are positive personality traits that:
  - ☐ Reflect personal identity (who you are);
  - ☐ Build positive outcomes for building well-being (e.g., health, relationships, peace) and managing adversity (e.g., increasing resilience, managing suffering, buffering against problems), when strengths are focused on and practiced.
  - ☐ Contribute to the greater good or collective good (e.g., to stronger families, groups, teams, cities, and societies).
- This research greatly expands outdated notions that personality is unchanging and cast in stone, and outdated notions of character as monolithic (e.g., only a handful of traits matter for everyone); singular (e.g., character = honesty and integrity only); all-or-none (e.g., you have character or you don't); and reputation-based (e.g., people are good or bad).

Character strengths and signature strengths

- Character strengths can be developed. It is likely that most people can enhance their capacity for expressing each of the 24 character strengths.
- Studies have shown that using one's signature strengths (i.e., your top strengths) in a new and unique way is an effective intervention: it has been shown to increase happiness and decrease depression for at least 6 months. The use of signature strengths has been found to be beneficial in different settings, including work and education.
- Deploying one's signature strengths at work is linked with greater work satisfaction, greater well-being, and higher meaning in life. Expressing four or more signature strengths at work is linked with more positive work experiences and meaningful work.
- Two of the most important predictors of employee retention and satisfaction are: reporting you use your top strengths at work and reporting that your immediate supervisor recognizes your top strengths.
- Research has found there is a strong connection between well-being and the use of signature strengths, because signature strengths help us make progress on our goals, allow us to express our true passion and meet our basic needs for autonomy, relationship, and competence.
- Practitioners who focus on a client's strengths immediately prior to a session increase strength activation, improve outcomes, foster a sense of mastery for the client, and strengthen the practitioner–client relationship.
- Character strengths buffer people from vulnerabilities (e.g., perfectionism and need for approval) which can play an important role in managing depression and anxiety.

Mindfulness-Based Strengths Practice (MBSP)
Reading Activity 2.2: VIA Classification of Character Strengths

Wisdom

Creativity: Originality; adaptive; ingenuity
Curiosity: Interest; novelty seeking; exploration; openness to experience
Judgment: Critical thinking; thinking things through; open-mindedness
Love of learning: Mastering new skills & topics; systematically adding to knowledge
Perspective: Wisdom; providing wise counsel; taking the big picture view

Courage

Bravery: Valor; not shrinking from fear; speaking up for what's right
Perseverance: Persistence; industry; finishing what one starts
Honesty: Authenticity; integrity; telling the truth
Zest: Vitality; enthusiasm; vigor; energy; feeling alive and activated

Humanity

Love: Both loving and being loved; valuing close relations with others
Kindness: Generosity; nurturance; care; compassion; altruism; "niceness"
Social intelligence: Aware of the motives and feelings of self and others

Justice

Teamwork: Citizenship; social responsibility; loyalty
Fairness: Being just; not letting feelings bias decisions about others
Leadership: Organizing group activities; encouraging a group to get things done

Temperance

Forgiveness: Mercy; accepting others' shortcomings; giving people a second chance
Humility: Modesty; letting one's accomplishments speak for themselves
Prudence: Careful; cautious; not taking undue risks
Self-regulation: Self-control; discipline; managing impulses & emotions

Transcendence

Appreciation of beauty and excellence: Awe; wonder; elevation; admiration
Gratitude: Thankful for the good; expressing thanks; feeling blessed
Hope: Optimism; future-mindedness; future orientation
Humor: Playfulness; bringing smiles to others; lighthearted
Spirituality: Purpose in life; meaning; calling; pursuit of the sacred

Session 3: Obstacles and Struggles Are Opportunities

Knowing is not enough; we must apply. Willing is not enough; we must do.

Goethe

A story to remember

Helen referred to herself as a notorious complainer about the weather. It was always too hot, too cold, too humid, too windy. Only about 1 or 2 days out of 365 was the weather "perfect" for her or "just right." She would often share her negative observations of the weather with her husband, friends, and children, which they were usually annoyed by, but had grown to tolerate. Through Helen's practice with mindfulness and character strengths, things began to change.

One day, she was walking down her long driveway to get the the mail from her mailbox and a sudden chilly breeze of wind hit her cheek. She thought to herself, "How dare the wind pick up pace right when I am coming outside for just a minute!" She started to get irritated as she did not have on warm clothes. She noticed her feeling arise and rather than cascading into frustration, she paused, closed her eyes and felt the coolness of the wind. She noticed how it offered a chill down her whole body. She used her curiosity to be open to it. She let go of the urge of her judgment/critical thinking strength to want to critique and interpret the wind as bad. She felt a sense of being connected to the wind, to nature. She then mindfully walked to her mailbox and back to her house. She was noticeably calm and even-tempered. She decided to make the weather an important part of her mindfulness practice. For Helen, the noticing of weather in any form – sun, hail, pouring rain, dark clouds – would be her cue to pause, be open and curious to what was present, and to see it for what it was. It was nature around her. As her practice with weather developed, she integrated additional character strengths including appreciating the beauty of all kinds of weather, having a sense of humor to laugh at herself when she went into judging mode about the weather, and feeling gratitude for her growing connection with nature.

A Strength-Based Mindfulness

Helen faced obstacles that had become so ingrained as a pattern in her that she was largely unaware of their expression and impact. As her mindfulness grew, she named her pattern (i.e., her weather obstacle) clearly. She became friendly with it. It was only then that she could transform it and actually appreciate it. It was no longer an obstacle, it was an opportunity for joy and connection with the world around her.

It is likely Helen would resonate with the following 13th-century Chinese koan:

In spring, hundreds of flowers;
in autumn, the harvest moon;
in summer, a refreshing breeze;
in winter, snow will be there with you.
If useless thoughts do not lurk in your mind any season is a good season for you.

We can all discover good seasons within us and outside of us.

You've spent time digging into your mindfulness, and you've spent time learning and exploring your character strengths. From this point forward, we'll explore the power around bringing mindfulness and character strengths together. This connection will help you develop your *growth mindset* – how you see problems, obstacles, and challenges as opportunities for growth. This means to use your perseverance and bravery to not avoid but to face and manage/overcome difficulties, your love of learning and curiosity to discover that each challenge has something to teach us, and your hope, gratitude, and zest to move forward in a way that is appreciative and accepting. Rather than feeling helpless in the face of a stressor or life conflict, you can tap into your mindfulness and strengths to see the stressor as a way to learn and develop.

Are you ready to take your mindfulness and strengths practices to the next level?

This chapter will explore ways you can use your strengths to help you with mindfulness. Any time we bring a character strength to improve an element of mindfulness, a meditation practice, or an aspect of mindful living, we are engaging in *strong mindfulness*. You will learn about and practice integrating character strengths to boost mindfulness in this chapter.

1. You'll build your understanding of why and how your signature strengths can influence your mindfulness practice.
2. You'll take steps to identify your meditation obstacles and make a plan you can implement right away for using your signature strengths to make progress in your mindfulness.

Together, these two areas help you to arrive at a place of greater confidence and comfort in handling mindfulness obstacles. We learn that *mindfulness without character strengths is purposeless and directionless* – character strengths provide energy, substance, and purpose. Character strengths direct our mindful attention to what is most important for us.

 YOUR MINDFUL PAUSE

Pause for a moment. Close your eyes and breathe for 15 seconds. Focus only on your in-breath and your out-breath.

Ask yourself: *Which of my character strengths might I bring forth right now?*

Take action with the character strength that rises strongest within you. This might be an action in your thinking, your words, or your actions – right now, or in your near future.

Using Character Strengths to Improve Your Meditation Practice

Let's be honest: Starting a meditation practice has its challenges, and keeping up a meditation practice can feel next to impossible for many people.

It's common to hear of individuals stopping their practice for one reason or another. This is because having a self-regulation practice of any kind is ripe with obstacles. Obstacles come in two forms: *internal* (thoughts like, "I can't do it" and body aches and pains) and *external* (like noises in the environment and logistic hurdles in scheduling times to practice).

Research on people who have participated in the structured program called *mindfulness-based strengths practice* (MBSP), there are many reasons given for not practicing meditation and mindfulness practices, but three come up most frequently:

- "I forgot to practice."
- "I'm too busy to practice."
- "My mind wandered too much."

The message of this chapter is that these and other obstacles are actually *opportunities* – for growth, for learning, for gaining insights, for changing perspective, for self-empowerment, and of course, for strengths use. So we'll turn here to learning how to break the common thought patterns that serve as barriers to your practice so you can take it to the next level.

Your character strengths are like deep wells of energy that can be accessed to help you get creative, enthusiastic, focused, and committed to your mindfulness practice. When you view and use your character strengths as the best parts of you, you'll be expressing those best parts in your practice.

Let's return to your top five signature strengths to see how they can energize your efforts in this regard. It's important to understand the rationale for why each strength can be helpful with your meditation practice. The following list offers rationale/example for each of the 24 character strengths within the VIA Classification:

- **Creativity** helps you consider an endless stream of ideas for making your practice successful.
- **Curiosity** helps you explore the present moment and countless stimuli you might notice.
- **Judgment/critical thinking** helps you balance the flow of emotions as you meditate.
- **Love of learning** helps you see the never-ending pool of knowledge and self-knowledge to explore through mindfulness.
- **Perspective** helps you see the bigger picture for yourself and your life as you reflect in meditation.

- **Bravery** helps you to confront challenges, to not avoid the difficult ups and downs of a meditation practice.
- **Perseverance** helps you stick with your practice when the going gets tough.
- **Honesty** helps you to see yourself more clearly in the way that you experience mindfulness.
- **Zest** helps you find excitement and energy when you really need it to keep your meditation practice joyful.
- **Love** offers warmth and care to a practice that sometimes has its harsh elements.
- **Kindness** helps to manage the self-critical part of your mind when you are meditating.
- **Social intelligence** helps you see, understand, and appreciate your many emotions that arise during meditation, and helps you be tuned into others' feelings during practices such as mindful listening..
- **Teamwork** helps you shift from a perspective of *I* to *we, you,* or *all beings,* as you meditate.
- **Fairness** helps you look deeply into issues of equality, suffering, and humanity during your meditation.
- **Leadership** helps you take initiative and enact important self-care as you build on your mindfulness.
- **Forgiveness** helps you in letting go of tension, thoughts, feelings – over and over throughout each practice.
- **Humility** helps you set aside your ego desires and wants, as you focus on your meditation.
- **Prudence** helps you plan your meditation experience and your meditation schedule.
- **Self-regulation** helps you return your attention to the present moment when it wanders off.
- **Appreciation of beauty & excellence** helps you notice the little things and value them in a mindful way.
- **Gratitude** helps you realize you can say "thank you" to any internal experience as you meditate.
- **Hope** helps you notice the positive amidst the discomfort that may arise when meditating.
- **Humor** helps you bring playfulness to your practice to balance excessive seriousness.
- **Spirituality** helps you embrace the sacred that every present moment brings.

Find your top five signature strengths in the list above. Read the example for each.

? How might these ways of thinking help you in your mindfulness practice? How might you put one or more of these examples into action?

_____

_____

_____

_____

_____

_____

_____

? Are there additional reasons your signature strengths can help you with your mindfulness practice? Write down other reasons here:

_____

_____

_____

_____

Now that you know a bit about *why* your signature strengths can be helpful in your meditation practice, you can start exploring *how* you might use your signature strengths in your mindfulness practice. Consider the specific ideas for merging strengths with mindfulness in the following list of action-oriented examples (some are actions of mind, some are actions of behavior) for each character strength:

- **Creativity:** Practice a variety of sitting, standing, and reclining postures, different ways to follow your breath, and alternate paths for managing mind wandering.
- **Curiosity:** Never stop exploring what is rising to the surface in your present moment. Then return your focus to your breath.
- **Judgment/critical thinking:** Investigate distractions that arise in your mind for several seconds before returning to your breath.
- **Love of learning:** Merge mindfulness with a meditation reading.
- **Perspective:** During meditation, periodically "zoom out" to gather a sense for your whole body, where you are sitting, and your existence within the larger world.
- **Bravery:** Keep challenging yourself! Gently challenge your body positioning (e.g., how you sit, how you cross your legs), breathe with muscle tension, face inner discomfort, and challenge yourself with the location of your practice – for example, with different types of weather, in loud and quiet environments.
- **Perseverance:** Challenge yourself at the onset of each meditation period to overcome one obstacle that arises – for example, mind wandering, sounds, body tension, etc. Keep going!
- **Honesty:** See each meditation experience as an opportunity to break through at least one internal blind spot to see yourself more clearly.
- **Zest:** Merge sitting meditation and mindful walking (e.g., walk, then sit, then walk).
- **Love:** Offer up each meditation experience as a loving dedication to someone alive or deceased; consider choosing a different person each time.
- **Kindness:** Weave in compassion practice (self-compassion and compassion for others) in each of your meditation practices.
- **Social intelligence:** For each meditation period, mindfully reflect on those who are suffering; empathize with the sufferer.
- **Teamwork:** Practice meditation with another person or as part of a meditation group or spiritual community.
- **Fairness:** Practice offering benefit to *include all beings* on the planet during your meditation (this includes humans, animals, plants, and other organisms).
- **Leadership:** In preparation for each new meditation period, organize a step-by-step structure that you'd be willing to follow.
- **Forgiveness:** Before each meditation, spend time deliberately letting go, in which you breathe out and release tension, stress, blame, and defensiveness.
- **Humility:** At the onset of your practice, remind yourself of the impermanence of life, your mortality, and the mortality of those you love.
- **Prudence:** Practice closely attending to every standard meditation instruction in your practice – for example, posture, airflow, placement of hands.
- **Self-regulation:** Follow a disciplined daily structure – same day, same time, same amount of time, same practice – for a week.
- **Appreciation of beauty & excellence:** Engage in your mindful sitting or mindful walking practice outside, with your eyes open.
- **Gratitude:** Infuse a blessing component at the beginning and end of your meditation practice.
- **Hope:** Practice your meditation during the day when your energy is highest; conclude with one optimistic statement.
- **Humor:** Prior to a meditation experience, prime yourself with playfulness by recalling one funny conversation or experience from the day.
- **Spirituality:** Infuse your mindfulness practice with an intention to connect with the sacred, the holy, or the transcendent within you and outside of you.

Find your five signature strengths in the list. Turn each of the examples into a practice phrase that you might take action with.

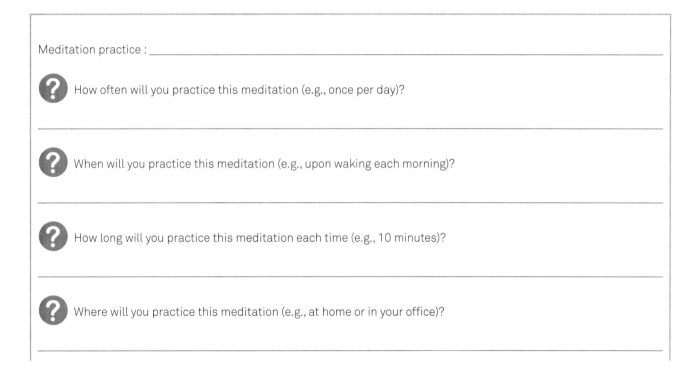 How *might* you bring each of these signature strengths into your mindfulness practice?

#1:_____

#2:_____

#3:_____

#4:_____

#5:_____

Map Out How You Will Bring Signature Strengths to Your Meditation Practice

Let's get more specific now. Name the meditation practice you want to make part of your routine (e.g., the Beginner's Mind Meditation on Audio Track 1, in Session 1, or the Character Strengths Breathing Space Meditation from Session 2, on Audio Track 4).

Meditation practice : _____

? How often will you practice this meditation (e.g., once per day)?

_____

? When will you practice this meditation (e.g., upon waking each morning)?

_____

? How long will you practice this meditation each time (e.g., 10 minutes)?

_____

? Where will you practice this meditation (e.g., at home or in your office)?

_____

Next, "catch" the internal and external obstacle(s) that most likely will get in the way of your practice. Check off at least one obstacle.

☐ My mind won't sit still.

☐ I'm too tired.

☐ I feel too much pain or discomfort.

☐ My mind is too negative.

☐ Too many bad memories pop up.

☐ I can't stop worrying.

☐ I'm too frustrated or upset.

☐ I'm never doing it well enough.

☐ I'm not making any progress.

☐ I don't see the point of meditation.

☐ I don't have time to practice.

☐ I forgot to practice.

☐ It is too hot or cold here, or too loud or quiet here.

☐ It's too boring. There's no pleasure in it.

If another obstacle comes to mind, note it here:

_____

_____

? How might you view your obstacle as an opportunity for growth and learning?

_____

_____

_____

_____

(?) How might you use your top signature strengths to overcome this obstacle? How will you bring strengths into your meditation experience to make it consistent and strong? Open yourself to the possibilities and explore them here?

Signature strength#1: _____

_____

Signature strength#2: _____

_____

Signature strength#3: _____

_____

Other strength: _____

_____

☼ DID YOU KNOW?

You can empower yourself to keep a strengths-based approach to mindfulness (Birtwell et al., 2019). Research shows there are four important steps to keep your mindfulness practice going strong:
1. practical resources (apps, books),
2. time and routine (a steady, frequent approach),
3. support from others (having a buddy or group),
4. positive attitudes and beliefs about the practice.

When difficulties arise in your mindfulness practice, why not see them as "par for the course" and a chance to use your signature strengths? Since every person experiences obstacles to meditation, know that they are to be expected. Taking this approach acknowledges and accepts your own imperfections, as well as the imperfect process of mindfulness.

To bring the insights from this chapter into your daily practice, try out the audio meditation (Mindful Breathing with Strengths) that will give you an additional lens for working with meditation obstacles and deepen your mindfulness. For one of the activities, you'll engage in an everyday experience that is ripe with challenges and in great need of your mindfulness and character strengths – your listening and speaking! Engaging in this activity will not only offer you unique opportunities for strengths use and

mindfulness application with obstacles, it will set you up for the next chapter's emphasis on mindful living. You'll also appreciate the character strengths of people in your life (an activity called Speak Up!), and discover new ways to bring mindful attention to your everyday life with the Strengths Mapping Activity.

Your MBSP Toolbox
Session 3: Obstacles and Struggles are Opportunities

Key Insights

- *Strong mindfulness* means using your character strengths to become more mindful. They can help you stick with a mindfulness practice, energize your actions and work, and help you to feel that you are bringing more of "you" into your mindfulness experiences.

- The most common reasons people struggle with mindfulness or meditation are thinking they are too busy, forgetting to practice, and reporting their mind wandered too much.

- After the naming of an obstacle, an opportunity arises to use one of your highest energy sources – your signature strengths – to help.

- Mindfulness without character strengths is purposeless. Character strengths provide energy, joy, authenticity, and purpose to mindfulness practices.

From the Science

- Research points to ways you can keep your strengths-based approach to mindfulness moving along: turn to books/ apps, have a formal plan each day for your practice, get support by doing the practice with others (e.g., tell people about your practice), and/or use your strengths to create a positive attitude about your practice (Birtwell et al., 2019).

For Your Exploration

- Why are each of your top 5 strengths important for your mindfulness practice?

- After you name one of your mindfulness obstacles, how might one of your signature strengths help you to stick with the practice or enjoy it more?

Pearl of Wisdom

- Microcosms inform the macrocosm: Difficulties in your mindfulness or strengths practice will arise; that is normal. How you handle those challenges might reflect how you handle any challenge in your life such as bigger stressors, relationship conflicts, and external pressures from work/school/finances. Consider your way of handling mindfulness/strengths obstacles as a microcosm for the greater macrocosm of your life.

Expand Your Toolbox

- Practice Mindful Breathing With Your Strengths (Audio Track 5): This meditation helps you energize your mindfulness practice by deliberately bringing your character strengths to the practice.

- Engage in mindful speaking and mindful listening (Practice Activity 3.1 and Practice Activity 3.2): These two mindful living activities help you to speak honestly from your heart and to be present to people in your life when they are communicating with you.

- Strength activity mapping (Practice Activity 3.3): This practice helps you discover the character strengths that you take for granted and are already present in your daily activities. It offers the opportunity to reignite strengths in your day.

Mindfulness-Based Strengths Practice (MBSP)
Activities and Tracking Sheet: Session 3

Suggested Activities for This Week

- Mindful Breathing with Strengths (Audio Track 5). Practice ×1/day.
- Character Strengths Breathing Space exercise (Audio Track 4). Continue this daily practice. Use it to face challenges in your day.
- Practice mindful listening and speaking this week on a least one day using Practice Activities 3.1 and 3.2.
- Speak Up! Tell two people about your appreciation of their strengths in action.
- Strengths-Activity Mapping (see Practice Activity 3.3).
- Track your meditation obstacles and experiences here and in your journal.

Day & date	Type of practice & time length	Obstacles to my practice	Strengths used	Observations & comments
Monday Date:				
Tuesday Date:				
Wednesday Date:				
Thursday Date:				
Friday Date:				
Saturday Date:				
Sunday Date:				

Audio Activities for Session 3

Track 5: Mindful Breathing With Strengths Meditation (Strong Mindfulness)

The focus of this meditation activity is to reinforce the importance of mindfulness of your breath AND to bring character strengths into your practice. Character strengths can help you overcome obstacles in your mindfulness practice and when focused on, can deepen and strengthen your mindfulness.

Practice Activities for Session 3

Practice Activity 3.1. Mindful Listening and Mindful Speaking

Improve your communication and your relationships by giving greater attention to your listening and speaking. Where is your mind when you are listening? Where is your mind when you are speaking? This activity will help you take a closer look so you can then take deliberate action with mindful speech and mindful listening.

Tips for My Mindful Listening

- When I am listening to someone, I will *be here now*.
- I will give my full attention – eyes and ears – to the speaker.
- I will set aside the impulse to react or to think of what I could say.
- I will use my character strengths to help me listen effectively.
- I will remember mindful listening means I will listen *imperfectly*.

Tips for My Mindful Speech

- When I am speaking, I will offer words that are honest and from the heart.
- I will speak in a way that is concise, specific, and direct.
- I will let go of speaking in tangents, disclaimers, hurtful comments, and repetitions.
- I will use my character strengths to help me speak with mindful care.
- I will remember mindful speaking means I will speak *imperfectly*.

Practice Activity 3.2. Monitoring and Practicing Mindful Listening and Mindful Speech

Look closer at your speech and listening. Monitor your communication and reflect on one example per day. Track and practice with your character strengths, noticing how they can give your mindfulness more depth and meaning.

Mindfulness-Based Strengths Practice (MBSP)
Practice Worksheet 3.1: Mindful Listening and Speaking Practice

		Mindful listening practice	
Day	Situation	Character strength(s) used	How I used the strength(s)
Example	Listening to my boss present to our team at lunch.	Curiosity; perseverance	I listened curiously, with an interest in new ideas. I was distracted by my mind's wandering to a family problem, so I persisted with my attention by bringing my attention back to listening with care.
1			
2			
3			
4			
5			
6			
7			

Mindful speaking practice			
Day	**Situation**	**Character strength(s) used**	**How I used the strength(s)**
Example	Speaking to my child after they broke a dish.	Honesty; social intelligence; kindness; forgiveness	I directly shared my upset feelings with my child. I was empathic to my child's feelings. I spoke in a caring way and shared my forgiveness.
1			
2			
3			
4			
5			
6			
7			

Practice Activity 3.3. Strengths-Activity Mapping

As most of us go about our day, we are unaware of the many ways we are using our character strengths in a particular moment. In other words, we are regularly mindless of our strengths use. And even though our signature strengths come naturally to us, this does not mean we're using them with attention and mindfulness. Often, we are missing opportunities, such as a chance to develop a strength amid a challenge, to use a strength in a discussion with someone else, or to handle a stressful moment with a strength.

You'll find that as you become more attentive to your character strengths, it opens the door to mindful living, to being open and curious about each task at hand. This activity will help you use your mindfulness to uncover and discover the strengths you are already using.

Steps

Choose one part of your day to focus on – a span in the morning, afternoon, or evening, whether you're at home, at school, at work, or anywhere in between. Set an alarm on your watch or smartphone to chime once or twice an hour during the time period you selected. Each time the alarm sounds, pause to write down in your journal your responses to the following:

1. What are you doing?
   - For example, e-mailing a friend, getting ready to take a walk, standing by the coffee machine, or setting the table for dinner.
2. Name at least one character strength you are using right now, however small, and how you're using it.
   - For example, *I'm using curiosity as I reflect on my day. I'm using love as I write out a birthday card. I'm using appreciation of beauty as I look at the trees around me.*
3. Name one obstacle that is getting in the way or could get in the way of your strengths use.
   - For example, you might note internal obstacles, such as fatigue, boredom, or self-criticism, or external obstacles, such as time demands, multitasking, or loud noises.
4. What might you do next?
   - For example, bring forth a different strength, overcome the obstacle with a strength, appreciate the strength you're already using.

Session 4: Strengthening Mindfulness in Everyday Life

In this life we cannot do great things. We can only do small things with great love.

Mother Teresa

A story to remember

"I have a trick I do!" exclaimed Roz to a few people in her small group. Roz had been practicing for a few weeks in a group that was developing their mindfulness and character strengths.

"When I'm on a long bus trip or subway trip, and I'm feeling bored, I do some secret strengths-spotting."

The group was intrigued. "What do you mean? What do you do?"

"Well, I privately look for the character strengths in others. I look at someone sitting across from me and I see that they are listening to music so I think they might be high in creativity. I see a young girl asking her mother a question and I realize the girl's curiosity. Someone reading a book beside me might be high in love of learning. A couple holding hands are using their strength of love, and the three teenagers telling stories and laughing are using their strengths of humor and zest. I go on and on like this in my mind. It's not about being right or wrong with what I see, it's about playing with strengths."

Roz continued: "As you know, I can be quite 'judgy' of others. I am quick to be critical of my kids and husband and sometimes I can look down on others. I am working on being more mindful and fair to others, their goodness, and seeing them more fully. This approach helps me become more balanced and truly mindful.

"Now, when I see a strength in someone, it makes my mindfulness stronger. It's like – I become more engaged in the moment, more attentive, more open and curious."

After listening to her, someone in the group noted: "That doesn't seem like a trick to me. That's a great practice. And one we can all do!"

Using Character Strengths to Positively Impact Your Mindful Living

In this chapter, like Roz, you'll continue on your journey of bringing character strengths to your mindful attention. The focus here will be on your daily life – your routines, your most basic activities and interactions. Each of these can be done with consciousness and with deliberate strengths use. This is referred to as *mindful living*.

Mindful living means to bring our energy of mindfulness into the various experiences of daily life. We take our routines and habits for granted. It's easy to give no attention to the trees and the blue sky and the feeling of the steering wheel in our hands while we're driving. It's easy to think about other things while someone else is talking. And it's commonplace to talk, read, and listen to music while we are eating. Mindless or inattentive living is the norm for most of us, most of the time.

But we can use all five of our senses to attend to these parts of our life. We can absorb the moment, cherish the moment, and live more in the moment. This is what it means to live mindfully, no matter what you're doing, no matter where or when.

Try the following activity and use the character strengths naturally flowing within you to support you with this mindfulness intention.

Mindfulness in Daily Living

1. Choose an area in which to practice mindful living. Let your strengths help you decide by choosing an activity that easily expresses your signature strengths. For example, people high in zest or appreciation of beauty may especially enjoy mindful walking, while people high in love of learning may relish mindful reading. Those high in love or kindness might be interested in mindful listening, while those high in social intelligence or honesty might be drawn to mindful speaking. Check one of the following:
   - ☐ Eating a meal
   - ☐ Eating a snack
   - ☐ Walking
   - ☐ Standing
   - ☐ Driving to work
   - ☐ Listening
   - ☐ E-mailing a friend
   - ☐ Creating a social media post
   - ☐ Playing
   - ☐ Speaking
   - ☐ Stretching and exercising
   - ☐ Reading

2. Experiment with this area. Practice bringing a careful, mindful attention to the activity while you do it.
   Remember that "mindful" describes the quality of action you are taking: It is action that engages all five senses (if possible), it proceeds slower than usual, and it repeatedly *returns* to the present moment.

3. After practicing mindful attention at least once with the activity you chose, pause to reflect: Which of your 24 character strengths were present as you engaged in the activity?

   For example, did you use prudence with each step as you practiced mindful walking? Appreciation of beauty with each bite as you engaged in mindful eating? Kindness to other drivers as you practiced mindful driving? Perspective (wisdom) as you practiced mindful listening each day with someone close to you? Remember, each of the 24 character strengths is possible with any mindful activity. List a few strengths along with how they were expressed during the activity.

Activity: _____

Strength: _____

How you expressed it: _____

_____

_____

_____

Strength: _____

How you expressed it: _____

_____

_____

_____

Strength: _____

How you expressed it: _____

_____

_____

_____

Strength: _____

How you expressed it: _____

_____

_____

_____

5. Now consider this: Any of your character strengths can infuse mindful living activities with more energy. They can bring you to higher levels of engagement and interest. Are there any character strengths you'd like to bring more deliberately into the activity? Think of it as bringing more of *you* into your daily life. Maybe you want to bring more creativity to your mindful e-mail correspondence? More prudence to your mindful driving? More zest to your mindful speaking? Jot down your strength intentions and how you'll bring them into your practice.

Activity: _____

Strength: _____

How you might express it: _____

_____

_____

_____

Strength: _____

How you might express it: _____

_____

_____

_____

Mindfulness With What You Dislike

Much of our daily living is filled with to-do lists, tasks, and activities that, at best, we find boring or, at worst, we highly dislike. There's the tediousness of things like vacuuming, sticking with bedtime routines, driving in traffic, homework. Then there are more challenging aspects to our day, like handling a tense moment with someone or having a difficult conversation.

 DID YOU KNOW?

Would you believe there was actually a study done on mindful dishwashing?! Two groups of dishwashers were compared. One group read a passage on a general dishwashing procedure. The other received instructions on mindful dishwashing.

The researchers found that those in the mindful group experienced increased inspiration, curiosity, and overall mindfulness, as well as decreased nervousness (Hanley et al., 2015).

The next time you wash dishes, use your five senses to be attentive to the temperature of the water, the weight of the dishes, and the smells in the air.

What all of these routines and stressful situations have in common is that we are not perceiving them as fully and completely as we can. We've all become locked into habit – a habitual way of reacting or behaving in the moment. But mindful attention helps you break that habitual pattern, and then adding your character strengths to the mix brings even more depth and dimension. Applied in unison, mindfulness and character strengths have the surprising potential to help you transform difficult situations into far more fulfilling experiences.

 YOUR MINDFUL PAUSE

Pause for a moment. Close your eyes and breathe for 15 seconds. Focus only on your in-breath and your out-breath.

Ask yourself: *Which of my character strengths might I bring forth right now?*

Take action with the character strength that rises strongest within you. This might be an action in your thinking, your words, or your actions - right now, or in your near future.

Let's experiment with these ideas.

? Consider an activity you dislike or that you find especially boring. Or, if you're feeling adventurous, consider a person to whom you dislike talking to. Write down the activity or the name of the person:

_____

_____

? What is the setting where you typically do this activity or speak with this person?

_____

_____

? Consider your top five signature strengths. What might you newly discover by using your best qualities?

_____

_____

_____

_____

_____

? Make note of other character strengths you might bring forth to support you. How will you use those strengths specifically in this situation?

_____

_____

_____

_____

_____

Remember, don't be afraid to learn from the opposite of mindfulness. As distractedness and mind wandering happen throughout the day, you can use your strengths to help you.

Let's say you want to become a more mindful parent. That's great. First, be honest with yourself with regard to one or two ways you are a mindless or distracted parent, such as when you are looking down at your smartphone when your child is showing you a picture they made in school....or when your child splashes a little bit of water out of the bathtub and you yell at them for it, unaware of the tension and anger you had been carrying. Distractedness and emotional tension are normal!

Moments of autopilot and mindlessness happen. We can learn from them. Perhaps you use your prudence strength and make a plan to leave your smartphone in a different room throughout the weekday evenings? This then gives you a greater chance you'll be less distracted and more attentive in the present moment. Perhaps you'll use your curiosity strength to question yourself as to how you are feeling throughout the day so you can notice troubling feelings earlier on; then perhaps you enlist forgiveness to let the feelings go, self-regulation to breathe with them, or bravery to investigate them further. Each of these strengths are examples that bring your mindfulness to the forefront and create a greater likelihood for mindful awareness in the short-run thereafter.

This chapter has focused on mindful living, bringing mindfulness and character strengths into the nuances of your daily life, your routines, and interactions. In the activities to work on this week, you'll practice with an aspect of living that we are quick to take for granted – movement and walking! Mindful walking is a powerful practice for building mindful attention, and your character strengths can help you. You're also invited to conduct a strength interview where you ask someone in your life a series of questions about their best qualities.

You'll discover the practice of strength gathas and mini-gathas. A gatha is a verse or set of phrases, that you pair with mindfulness to help you be present in the moment. These can be integrated into your day, because of their simplicity for memorizing and applicability across situations.

> ## Your MBSP Toolbox
> ## Session 4: Strengthening Mindfulness in Everyday Life
>
> **Key Insights**
>
> - *Mindful living* means to bring the present-moment energy of mindfulness and strengths into your daily routines and actions. This helps you to increase your enjoyment and peace in life. Paying attention to one thing at a time facilitates mindful living.
> - Your strengths also help you with mindful living. You might use prudence or zest when you walk mindfully, gratitude when you eat mindfully, kindness when you drive mindfully, and curiosity and social intelligence as you listen mindfully.
> - You can transform boring tasks (e.g., vacuuming, making your bed, folding laundry) by mindfully paying attention to your senses and to the novel features of the activity.
>
> **From the Science**
>
> - In a research study of people washing dishes mindfully (compared with people who washed dishes as usual), the mindful dishwashers experienced higher curiosity, inspiration, and overall mindfulness, and less nervousness (Hanley et al., 2015).
>
> **For Your Exploration**
>
> - What is something you want to improve on (e.g., parenting, working on a project)? Consider when you are particularly distracted when doing that activity (e.g., mindless parenting, mindless working). What is one small action you can take to be more present at that time? Which of your character strengths might help you?
>
> **Pearl of Wisdom**
>
> - Life is (re)discovered in the little things. Use your mindful attention and your character strengths to help you appreciate this reality.
>
> **Expand Your Toolbox**
>
> - Mindful Walking practice (Audio Track 6): Practice walking with your full attention. Engage your senses. Be aware of your inner experience and the external environment.
> - Conduct a Strengths Interview: Interview (Practice Activity 4.2) any person in your life about their character strengths – how they see the strengths in themselves, why they are important to them, and ways they use them during good and challenging times.
> - Use the strengths gatha meditation throughout your day. Say and image these phrases:
>   - Breathing in, I see my strengths,
>   - Breathing out, I value my strengths,
>   - Dwelling now in my strengths,
>   - I express myself fully.
> - Create your own strengths gatha to use in your daily life.

Mindfulness-Based Strengths Practice (MBSP)
Activities and Tracking Sheet: Session 4

Suggested Activities for This Week

- Mindful Walking Meditation (Audio Track 6). Practice ×1/day.
- Character Strengths Breathing Space exercise (Audio Track 4). Use this as needed to support your practice and your application of mindfulness and character strengths into daily life.
- Create a strengths gatha and use this as a short meditation (see Audio Track 7 and Practice Activity 4.1).
- Conduct a strengths interview with a family member, friend, or colleague (Practice Activity 4.2).
- Track your mindfulness practices, including mindful walking, eating, driving, etc., here or in your journal.

Day & date	Type of practice & time length	Obstacles to my practice	Strengths used	Observations & comments
Monday Date:				
Tuesday Date:				
Wednesday Date:				
Thursday Date:				
Friday Date:				
Saturday Date:				
Sunday Date:				

Audio Activities for Session 4

Track 6: Mindful Walking Meditation

This practice will help you bring attention to something that is easily taken for granted – walking and movement. Mindful walking involves paying attention to each step and movement. Attention is placed on both what is happening inside oneself (e.g., feelings, body's balance) and outside oneself (e.g., visuals, sounds). Character strengths are attended to as a pathway to become more mindful and to deepen the experience.

Track 7: Strengths Gatha

The concept, examples, practical applications, and reflections for the strengths gatha meditation (and activity) are described in detail in Practice Activity 4.1. It is also useful to listen and experience this brief audio track.

Practice Activities for Session 4

Practice Activity 4.1. Strengths Gathas

One of the best ways to be more deliberate about bringing mindfulness and character strengths into your daily life – into any activity – is by developing and using strengths *gathas*.

"Gatha" is a Sanskrit term meaning song, poem, or verse. Gathas were popularized by the renowned mindfulness teacher Thich Nhat Hanh. They are intended to create an awareness in the present moment *and* a connection with the immediate future based on their content. Gathas differ from mantras, in which individuals repeat a phrase, word, or sound with the intention of creating a state of relaxation or oneness. In contrast, gathas help to catalyze moments of mindful living and positive actions for the immediate future.

Steps

1. Choose a character strength (e.g., gratitude) or choose a mindfulness or character strength concept (e.g., mindful eating or your signature strengths) to focus on.

2. Create a short gatha (two to four lines) that captures the essence of the character strength or concept you are targeting.
3. Weave elements of mindfulness practice into the gatha, as appropriate (such as breathing, walking, slowing down, deepening awareness, clear seeing, widening perspective, using your senses, facing challenges in the now, and so on).
4. Memorize and practice your strengths gatha each day.

Two Examples of Strengths Gathas

Breathing in, I see my strengths,
Breathing out, I value my strengths,
Dwelling now in my strengths,
I express myself fully.

Breathing in, I see my fear,
Breathing out, I bow to my bravery,
Remembering to call it forth,
I grow my capacity.

Write your strength gatha here:

_____

_____

_____

_____

How might you bring this gatha forth during your day?

_____

_____

_____

_____

Need more examples of gathas? Consider the following section, Strength Mini-Gathas, which offers 24 strength mini-gathas, which you can pair with one breath! With your inhale you say the character strength and with your exhale you say one phrase. They are even easier to memorize and bring into your daily life. This idea was inspired by the poetic work of Thich Nhah Hanh (2009) and Mary Oliver (2017).

Examples: Strength Mini-Gathas

Breathing in – creativity; Breathing out – I see another way.

Breathing in – curiosity; Breathing out – what will I notice?

Breathing in – judgment; Breathing out – the details matter.

Breathing in – love of learning; Breathing out – knowledge is power.

Breathing in – perspective; Breathing out – stepping back.

Breathing in – bravery; Breathing out – I can do this.

Breathing in – perseverance; Breathing out – keep going.

Breathing in – honesty; Breathing out – be myself.

Breathing in – zest; Breathing out – energy flowing through me.

Breathing in – love; Breathing out – I offer a hug.

Breathing in – kindness; Breathing out – how may I help?

Breathing in – social intelligence; Breathing out – I feel for you.

Breathing in – teamwork; Breathing out – you and I together.

Breathing in – fairness; Breathing out – I'm OK, you're OK.

Breathing in – leadership; Breathing out – I see your strengths.

Breathing in – forgiveness; Breathing out – I let go.

Breathing in – humility; Breathing out – I release my-self.

Breathing in – prudence; Breathing out – pausing to think.

Breathing in – self-regulation; Breathing out – I feel my outbreath.

Breathing in – appreciation of beauty & excellence; Breathing out – how wonderful!

Breathing in – gratitude; Breathing out – thank you.

Breathing in – hope; Breathing out – I see the good.

Breathing in – humor; Breathing out – smile, levity.

Breathing in – spirituality; Breathing out – I see the sacred.

Practice Activity 4.2. Strengths Interview

Ready to immediately improve one of your relationships? Whether it's someone you just met or someone very close to you, the strengths interview is a great opportunity to deepen your connection and give them a boost of well-being along the way.

Steps

1. Choose one person to interview about their strengths.
2. Plan out a way to explain the activity to them.
   Example:
   - "I am spending more time focusing on what is strongest in myself and in the people around me. I would like to learn about your strengths and how they connect with who you are, as well as with your past successes. Thank you for your willingness to explore this with me."
3. List the questions you want to ask.
   Examples:
   - What was one of the best experiences of your professional (or personal) life – a time when you felt most alive, engaged, and proud of your work?
     - What character strengths did you notice in the story you just shared with me?
   - What are your *highest* strengths of character?
   - How have you used your strengths to *overcome* adversity and stress in your life?
   - During a typical day, when do you feel most *energetic* and *alive*?
     - What are the *little things* in life that matter most to you?
     - Which of your strengths contribute to these?
   - What *engages* you most – or connects you most with the present moment?
     - What activities give you the most *pleasure*?
     - What gives you a sense of *meaning* and purpose? How often do you tap into that experience of meaning?
     - How might your strengths help you to search for or discover meaning?

Tips

- Approach the interview with a beginner's mind – listening to the person's responses as if you are hearing them for the first time, with a sense of newness and freshness, fully tuned in.
- Allow the interview to take on a life of its own. Remember that this is someone you have a relationship with;

we cannot control relationships, so just *allow* the interaction to unfold.

- Keep the focus on the other person. You can make time to share your own story and feedback, if you wish, following the interview.

- Practice mindful listening. When your mind wanders or you lose track of what to ask, trust in yourself (return to your breath, return to your strengths).

- If the person shifts to speaking of the negative, dwelling on what went wrong, or going off on tangents, shift the focus back to strengths.

? Who will you interview?

_____

? How do you plan to approach them?

_____

_____

? What are some of the questions you'll ask to help them explore and share about their character strengths?

_____

_____

_____

_____

_____

_____

_____

_____

? What character strengths will you need to turn to as the interviewer (e.g., curiosity in your tone of voice, gratitude as you appreciate their efforts to speak with you, or bravery to encourage the person to keep exploring something they may not be accustomed to talking about)?

_____

_____

_____

Session 5:
Your Relationship With Yourself and Others

I want to hold the hand inside you,
I want to take the breath that's true.

Hope Sandoval
(from the band, Mazzy Star)

A story to remember

"I have to tell you something that happened during my mindfulness practice this month." These words were spoken by a young woman with chronic pain whom I had been working with for several months, offering a variety of pain management practices, including mindfulness meditation. She had suffered much over the years but was trying her best to cope with her pain and create a new life for herself.

"OK, great, I'd love to hear it."

"So, I was practicing mindfulness. I was trying to be more friendly in my practice. I started to be gentle with myself and suddenly I realized I had not ever been friendly with myself. I've seen my body as something that's wrong because it is often in pain. I need to be a better friend to myself. In fact, I need to become my own best friend to myself."

"This seems like an incredible insight," I remarked, "to become your own best friend."

"Yes, friends treat one another with respect, and they look out for one another. They listen and are there for one another. That's how I am going to be with myself going forward."

After a pause, I asked, "And in what way are your character strengths part of this insight?"

"I've thought about how it's not fair that I am so young and having to be in pain and having these medical issues. But, it is also true that I need to be fair to myself now, and to what my body needs now. It is not fair for me to be degrading or negative on my body, or to infuse it with unhealthy food or drink. I don't deserve that. I also see forgiveness. I can forgive myself for doing too much activity and for not listening to my body very well in the past. Now it is time for me to be loving and gentle with myself, just like a best friend would."

Impact Your Relationships

Mindful appreciation and mindful strengths use extends to our relationships. Research has found over and over that an essential element of well-being, perhaps the most important one, is having close relationships that are positive. If there's one thing that's clear, it's that our relationships matter a lot.

The concepts we'll cover in this chapter – strengths recognition, strengths appreciation, and hot buttons – can apply to any of our relationships: with a boss, coworkers, neighbors, our significant other, child(ren), parents, friends, teammates, and your relationship with yourself,

as the young woman in the opening story pointed out. The focus here will be on *close* relationships – those that matter most to us and fill us with the most meaning, comfort, and love. This chapter will help you deepen those relationships with mindful strengths use and appreciation.

Character strengths use without mindfulness is hollow. Mindfulness give your character strengths greater depth and breadth. That carries substantial weight in the area of our relationships.

One of the most remarkable findings on the integration of mindfulness and character strengths (the MBSP, or mindfulness-based strengths practice program) is the impact it has on relationships. People find that relationships that have been neglected or damaged can be improved, and their current relationships can also benefit and grow from the work.

Mindful and Mindless Expressions of Strengths in Relationships

If you want to strengthen your close relationships, a useful first step is starting to recognize when and how you are operating on *autopilot* in your communication – in other words, when you are speaking/behaving out of distractedness and habit rather than speaking/behaving with presence and awakeness. Remember, we can appreciate that our autopilot mind is beneficial in multiple ways: It gets us through everything we need to accomplish in a day, it operates in the background so we can concentrate on other topics, and it has been shown to boost efficiency and productivity. But if we are on autopilot too much of the time when we are with others, our relationships with them will suffer.

To illustrate this, let's look through the lens of your top five strengths, your *signature strengths*. When you give them little attention and take them for granted, you're not being fully present. It is easy to take our signature strengths for granted because we use them frequently and automatically. The examples that follow aren't meant to imply that people express their best qualities on autopilot *all* of the time or that they're intentionally being uncaring or negligent in any way. Rather, these examples might catalyze awareness and insight about interactions in relationships to support mindful, strengths-based living.

New Opportunities: Overcome the Taking-Strengths-For-Granted Effect

Any of the 24 character strengths can be taken for granted and be expressed in a superficial way. In many cases, the strength is barely there, devoid of much meaning, connection, or mindful attention. Consider these examples:

- When you think to yourself: "I don't really feel like answering your question so I'll just say the first thing that comes to my mind" (creativity on autopilot).
- "That's interesting," you passively say to your friend's story about their day and then you move on to talk about your day (curiosity on autopilot).

- "No, I don't think so," you say without giving your spouse's idea any time for reflection (judgment on autopilot).
- When at the bookstore (or when buying online) you say to yourself, "I'll get this one and this one, and this one looks interesting, I'll get that too" (love of learning on autopilot).
- "It sounds like you have a cough. You should go to the doctor" (perspective on autopilot).
- When asked, "Who wants to dive in?"; without thinking you say, "I will" (bravery on autopilot).
- "Yes, I'll get it done" or "I'm working on it" as a response to someone asking you about a task that you are struggling with (perseverance on autopilot).
- In a situation where someone asks you what was said about them (and you know it was all negative comments), you say, "I'm not exactly sure what they said. I don't recall it word-for-word" (honesty on autopilot).
- Showing a mind–body mismatch where you greet someone with a big "hello, how are you doing!?" but your body is tired and unexpressive (zest on autopilot).
- A quick "OK, love you" as you leave home giving a kiss on your loved one's cheek (love on autopilot).
- After a neighbor tells you of the death of one of their relatives, you quickly say to them, "I'm sorry for your loss" (kindness on autopilot).
- "Hey, how are you doing today?" or "What's up with you?" and then you don't listen for the response, and you start talking about what you wanted to say all along (social intelligence on autopilot).
- "We're a good team," you passively say when someone comments on the good work done at your place of employment (teamwork on autopilot).
- "OK, play fair. Be sure to share," you passively say to your child as they go outside to play (fairness on autopilot).
- The manager who walks passed their employees each day, and their one interaction is to make the comment, "Good work, everyone" (leadership on autopilot).
- When someone apologizes to you for a wrongdoing and you quickly say, "That's OK. It's OK" and nothing else (forgiveness on autopilot).
- Someone goes out of their way to give you a compliment, and you respond, "Oh, it's no big deal" (humility on autopilot).
- "Stick with the plan, just do what we always do" (prudence on autopilot).
- "I'm not feeling anything. I didn't feel anything when she said that to me" (self-regulation on autopilot).
- "Beautiful job on that drawing," the parent says to their child and then begins focusing on how they got three

answers wrong on their math assignment (appreciation of beauty and excellence on autopilot).

- An almost imperceptible "Great, thanks" when in conversation with a work colleague (gratitude on autopilot).
- "I hope you feel better" and no explanation or further comments are offered (hope on autopilot).
- "That's funny," you say to your friend with a fake smile and forced laugh at their story (humor on autopilot).

- Before eating dinner, you "say grace" (or offer another prayer or words of devotion) without even realizing you are saying the words or what their intended meaning is (spirituality on autopilot).

In each of the above examples, the intention is likely good. It's that the expression is hollow. There's not much there. Mindful awareness is needed to give greater depth and connection to the person or issue at hand.

? Do you relate to these examples? Any of your 24 character strengths can go on autopilot in your interactions with others. To explore this further, start by considering which of your signature strengths come across on autopilot in your relationships? How so?

_____

_____

_____

_____

_____

Although it is entirely normal and common to communicate in autopilot mode, it doesn't benefit the other person or show much of a connection to them. And because this is so prevalent in our everyday speech and behaviors, we're often not even aware when we're speaking and acting mindlessly. But what would happen if we _were_ aware, if we used our strengths mindfully in our relationships?

When you're fully present and paying close attention to your communication, the interaction is transformed. The following list offers examples of how the 24 character strengths can be mindfully expressed in the same scenarios offered earlier:

- "As I think about your question, there are three different directions I could take to answer it. My answer is going to connect all three together and perhaps still be of help to you!" (mindful creativity).
- "That's interesting. Tell me more about what happened at work. What was most impactful about what your boss said to you?" (mindful curiosity).
- "My first instinct is to say that that won't work, but let me think this through a bit more. I'll give it some more thought, and I'll get back with you on that soon" (mindful judgment).

- When buying books, you say to yourself, "There are so many topics I want to dig into and learn about. I'll start with this one here and really absorb everything I can" (mindful love of learning).
- "I've been hearing that cough of yours for a while now. You look a bit pale as well. I know there are a lot of sicknesses going around in our area. Do you think it might be good to get yourself checked out?" (mindful perspective).
- When asked, "who wants to dive in?" you say, "that looks a bit risky, but if no one else volunteers I'm happy to jump in as long as I have some support from others" (mindful bravery).
- "I'm struggling with this task, but I'm working hard on it. I can see several different problems with it, but I also see the steps I need to take. I will get this finished" (mindful perseverance).
- "They said some unkind words about you. Would you like me to say more about that? I can share with you the details of what I recall, but I know it might be hurtful for you to hear" (mindful honesty).
- Your body language, smile, and words are at the same level of enthusiasm and engagement as you greet someone with "what's going on?" (mindful zest).

- "I love you, ___," and you feel the sensation of your lips touch the cheek of your loved one. You deliberately hug the person for an extra few seconds while feeling the contact of the warm embrace (mindful love).
- After a neighbor tells you of a death of one of their relatives, you say to them, "Oh, I'm so sorry, Jon. I know how much your aunt meant to you. I am here for you. What can I help you with?" You then take action in some way, by not only offering to help but actually helping them, such as bringing them a dinner or writing them a thoughtful letter (mindful kindness).
- "Hey, how are you doing? I was thinking about you the other day. How did everything go with that conversation with your boss earlier this week?" (mindful social intelligence).
- "The project was a success because of all five of us communicating and working together each day. Here's what each person did...." (mindful teamwork).
- "When you share your toys with friends it makes them feel happy. It is a way to include others who might feel left out. That is a fair way to behave. What do you think about that idea?" (mindful fairness).
- The manager pauses at a different employee's desk each morning. They make a personal comment about the person and their work, for example, "Amal, I want to let you know that I've noticed the quality time and effort you've been putting in on the projects these last 2 weeks. You've shown strong perseverance and teamwork." (mindful leadership).
- When someone apologizes to you for a wrongdoing, you say, "Thank you for apologizing. I was hurt by you when you did that to me. I felt quite upset. But I am moving on, and I want you to know that I forgive you. I forgive you for what you did and the pain you brought to me. I'm letting it go. I hope you will let it go, too" (mindful forgiveness).
- Someone goes out of their way to give you a compliment, and you say, "I appreciate your thoughtful observation. I simply tried to do my best on that project, and it was rewarding to complete it and do so with such a great group. Have you had an experience lately that was rewarding as well?" (mindful humility).
- "I like the plan we have set up for our morning routine each week. Would it be OK with you if we stuck to that plan, and then, if we have some extra time, we can do the additional activity you mentioned?" (mindful prudence).
- "I felt sad that she would actually say that to me. After all, we are friends. I also felt angry because she said it in front of the class. That was embarrassing" (mindful self-regulation).

- "Wow, look at that drawing you created. The blues and greens are so striking! And I see so many precise designs in your picture. This is quite beautiful. I'm enjoying admiring all the details here!" (mindful appreciation of beauty and excellence).
- "Judy, I wanted to take a moment to tell you how much I appreciated all the effort you made on this project especially considering all that you have going on right now in your life. You really went the extra mile. I'm grateful to you for your hard work" (mindful gratitude).
- "I know you've been under a lot of stress these last couple weeks. I really hope you feel better and that you get some time for some exercise, as I know you love that. I am confident you'll make some time for yourself this week!" (mindful hope).
- "That's hysterical, I can't believe you said that to him!" you say as you belly laugh at your friend's funny story, "now I've got a great story to tell you...." (mindful humor).
- Before eating dinner, you turn to your heart and express appreciation for the food and the connection with the people you are with (mindful spirituality).

In these situations, both mindful awareness and mindful strengths use are present. Mindfulness serves as a mechanism that activates a much deeper level of relating, one that is represented through the thoughtful and genuine expression of character strengths.

Do you relate to these examples of mindful strengths use? Why or why not?

_____

_____

_____

_____

Choose two of your signature strengths. How might you express these in your relationships, with greater mindful attention? With whom will you use your strengths? How will your use of them be more mindful?

Character strength: _____

Person: _____

Mindful strength use: _____

_____

Character strength: _____

Person: _____

Mindful strength use: _____

YOUR MINDFUL PAUSE

Pause for a moment. Close your eyes and breathe for 15 seconds. Focus only on your in-breath and your out-breath.

Ask yourself: *Which of my character strengths might I bring forth right now?*

Take action with the character strength that rises strongest within you. This might be an action in your thinking, your words, or your actions - right now, or in your near future.

Mindful Recognition of Relationship Hot Buttons

Our relationships are often a source of tension. When we become upset during an encounter, we often react without much thought, and before we know it, a disagreement becomes an argument, or a misinterpretation becomes a conflict. It's common to be triggered in your close relationships, so you may have already explored your feelings of anger, sadness, and fear that play a part in conflicts (if not, a mindful, gentle exploration of your feelings and what is being triggered within you can be very beneficial). It's far less probable, however, that you've explored the role of character strengths in relationship disharmony.

Sometimes our character strengths affect our perception of an experience or an exchange – it can bother us when others don't express strengths as we do. For example, it can be upsetting when a person does not express fairness to a particular group of people, kindness in support of an important cause, or reciprocal curiosity in asking us how our day was when we showed interest in theirs. On the flip side, someone can express too much of a character strength, like a display of spirituality or zest that appears over-the-top and out of proportion to the situation; that can leave us feeling annoyed or affronted. When something related to character strengths is triggered in us, that's referred to as a strength *hot button*.

Let's explore this a bit further.

Choose one of your close relationships and name that person here:

_____

Specify a situation that has come up more than once with this person that seems to trigger you, to the point where you feel mildly or moderately upset, offended, or hurt.

_____

_____

_____

(?) What character strength is being triggered in you in some way? How so?

_____

_____

_____

(?) To build a new understanding around this hot button issue, consider: What might you do differently next time? What other character strengths could you bring forth to bring comfort or balance to your feelings? Or what strengths might you need to express more in this relationship?.

_____

_____

_____

_____

Understanding your strength hot buttons can help you navigate the challenges of relationships and more easily access the rewards of those relationships.

Mindful Appreciation of Strengths in Others

You can take your insights on improving your own autopilot strengths use to the next level by applying them to others. We can show the people we care about that we really do see them for who they are, that we notice their best or ideal self. That starts with strengths awareness and continues with strengths appreciation.

To recognize and express value for another person's strengths reaps significant benefits. Research on intimate relationships confirms that couples who recognize and appreciate the best character strengths in each other experience greater happiness in their relationship, a greater sense of both belonging and independence, higher sexual satisfaction, and greater relationship commitment. That's quite promising news about a simple process we can embed right now into our conversations with loved ones!

The trouble is, we take our relationships for granted. Instead of showering (or even "drizzling") the people we're closest to with appreciation, we allow our connections to operate on autopilot all too often. But you can counteract this tendency by creating a good relationship habit marked by character strengths and mindfulness.

Follow these steps:

1. Pick one of your closest relationships and identify three of that person's top character strengths. They don't have to have taken the VIA Survey themselves (though it would certainly be helpful, if they're interested in doing so) – you can identify some of their top strengths based on your knowledge of them and their day-to-day behaviors.

   List three character strengths that this person expresses often:

   Strength #1: _____

   Strength #2: _____

   Strength #3: _____

2. Write down a recent example of when this person admirably displayed each of these strengths.

   ? How did you see the strength expressed?

   Example for strength #1: _____

   Example for strength #2: _____

   Example for strength #3: _____

3. Now read what you wrote about this person's strengths to them, explaining why their character strength use is important to you and valued by you. (And don't worry if they wouldn't pick the same three top strengths for themselves that you did. No one ever says, "No, that's not a correct strength for me" or "I don't want that strength." On the contrary, most people are just extremely touched that mindful attention is being devoted to them.) For example, their use of character strengths may make you feel more emotionally attracted to them, more committed to the relationship, more connected in friendship, or happier to be around them. Appreciation can also be expressed nonverbally.

   ? How did you (or will you) express appreciation for this person's strengths use?

   _____

   _____

   _____

   _____

Understanding how your character strengths interact with those of others is interrelated with mindful characters strengths use. As you practice spotting the strengths of others you notice how your own strengths use impacts others. You can apply the components of mindfulness – self-regulation and openness – to support you in reducing tension and elevating positivity in all of your relationships.

💡 **DID YOU KNOW?**

In Session 4, you practiced creating and using strengths gathas to bring mindfulness and strengths into your daily life. Well, you can also create a *relationship gatha* to improve your intimacy and connectedness with your partner, family member, friend, co-worker, or neighbor.

This will help you bring more mindfulness and strengths to the present moment as well as to the immediate future as you enhance your appreciation of the person. The first line of this gatha brings us to break through strengths blindness to become mindful that the individual is a person of strengths (you "see" them). The second line helps us appreciate the strengths of the person. The third line gives us a validation of our strengths-spotting and gives it a tangible quality. The fourth line points to the deepening of connection with the person. You can apply this gatha when you are alone while thinking of the person, or while sitting with them:

> Breathing in, I see your strengths,
> Breathing out, I value your strengths,
> Sensing now your strengths,
> I connect with you.

❓ Who might you think about for this strengths gatha?

_____

❓ What is a situation that you most appreciated when you were with them?

_____

_____

_____

_____

? After you experience the meditation directed toward them, explore your feelings. What was it like to do this activity? How did you feel?

_____

_____

_____

_____

_____

? Bonus challenge: Consider a person in your life who you have some conflict or difficulty with. Despite the problem(s) with the person, you know you do care about or you want to collaborate with them better. Experiment with applying the lines of this gatha toward them. Write about your experience in approaching this activity, in doing the activity, and your feelings afterward.

_____

_____

_____

_____

_____

_____

By working through the exercises in this session, you've made a powerful start in developing greater mindful strengths use and appreciation in your relationships. This creates a positive foundation for your relationships to continue to grow, and pathways for ongoing nurturance of them. Solidify that foundation even more by listening to the Loving-Gratitude Meditation (Audio Track 8) and/or the Strength-Exploration Meditation (Audio Track 9) this week. And, the Character Strengths 360 activity will bring your character strengths awareness and strengths potential to new heights!

> **⚒ Your MBSP Toolbox**
> **Session 5: Your Relationship With Yourself and Others**

Key Insights

- Character strengths use without mindfulness is hollow. Mindfulness gives your character strengths greater depth and breadth.
- You can overcome the "taking strengths for granted effect" in your life by infusing any strengths use with mindful attention.
- Any of your character strengths can be turned outward to bring benefit to another person.

From the Science

- Scientists have found that when couples recognize and appreciate the character strengths of their partner they are more likely to experience greater relationship satisfaction, sexual satisfaction, relationship commitment, and report that their needs were met (Kashdan et al., 2017).

For Your Exploration

- What is one example of how you take your character strengths for granted?
- How might you bring greater mindful attention to this example?

Pearl of Wisdom

- When you spot the character strengths of a person in your life, it is like you are making a delicious cake the two of you can enjoy *together*. But, be sure to convey your appreciation for the person's strengths – why you value their strengths – as that is the chocolate that goes on the cake.

Expand Your Toolbox

- Turn your strengths gatha outward. You can slightly change the words in a strengths gatha to be directed toward another person. Try saying/imaging a gatha with another person in mind; this can add new positive dimensions to your perception of them.
- Practice the Loving-Gratitude Meditation (Audio Track 8). This practice helps you rediscover, connect with, and cultivate the strengths of love and gratitude within you.
- The Character Strengths 360 (Practice Activity 5.1): Give this short survey to several people in your life, asking them to take a few minutes to point out 5 of your highest character strengths and examples of each. Look at the patterns of strengths that others spotted in you. Examine your highest strengths on the Character Strengths 360 alongside your highest strengths on the VIA Survey. This will add new insights to how you see yourself.

Mindfulness-Based Strengths Practice (MBSP)
Activities and Tracking Sheet: Session 5

Suggested Activities for This Week

- Loving-Gratitude Meditation (Audio Track 8) and/or the Strength-Exploration Meditation (Audio Track 9). Practice ×1/day or also consider alternating between the two each day.
- Distribute the Character Strengths 360 activity (Practice Worksheet 5.1) to people in your life. Gather their feedback and examine and track the results for patterns and personal insights (Practice Worksheet 5.2).
- Complete the Character Strengths Brainstorm worksheet, on one of your strengths (Practice Activity 5.2).
- Track your experiences here or in your journal.

Day & date	Type of practice & time length	Obstacles to my practice	Strengths used	Observations & comments
Monday Date:				
Tuesday Date:				
Wednesday Date:				
Thursday Date:				
Friday Date:				
Saturday Date:				
Sunday Date:				

Audio Activities for Session 5

Track 8: Loving-Gratitude Meditation

We can build our relationship with ourselves through a practice of mindfulness, as well as with a focus on specific character strengths. The first meditation on loving-gratitude is centuries old. It involves first imaging a time when you felt deeply and genuinely loved, imaging the person who was offering you this love, feeling this in your body in the present moment, allowing yourself to feel grateful for the loved one and feel that gratitude in your body, and then stating four meditation phrases to reinforce the strength of love and also gratitude.

Track 9: Strength-Exploration Meditation

This meditation provides an opportunity to focus on one strength – to simply follow your breathing and image one strength of your choice; you can then monitor your body and mind, moment to moment, taking notice of what occurs in relation to this strength. This meditation can be helpful if you wish to further understand or develop one of your character strengths. It involves using mindfulness to observe your moment-to-moment experience as you "sit with" the strength.

Practice Activities for Session 5

Practice Activity 5.1. Character Strengths 360

The Character Strengths 360 activity is one of the most cherished and insight-generating activities in the field of character strengths. This is because it gives you the opportunity to learn about yourself through the eyes of others. As human beings, we have many blinds spots about ourselves, especially our character strengths. This activity provides you a special opportunity.

Ask several people in your life, across your life domains (family, work, social) to complete this activity on your behalf. This involves their naming the strengths they see highest in you (ideally limiting to five strengths) and sharing an example of how you expressed that strength (see Practice Worksheet 5.1). One way you can track the strengths feedback is to use Practice Worksheet 5.2 to check off the character strengths each person spotted in you and to observe them next to your VIA Survey results.

As you examine the results together, from the VIA Survey and the various Character Strengths 360s you gather, you might notice that there are three main categories that offer particularly helpful insights:

1. Strong signature strengths: those strengths noted as high by both you and others (the strength is in the top 5–7 on both).
2. Possible blind spots: those strengths noted as high by others only (top 5–7 on the 360 but not the VIA Survey), thus representing areas that you might be "blind" to or less aware of.
3. Potential opportunities: those strengths noted as high by you only (top 5–7 on the VIA Survey but not the 360), thus representing avenues of future expression with others.

As you begin to distribute this activity to others, consider the following helpful tips:

- You can tell people it generally takes 5–10 minutes to fill out.
- Strongly encourage people to write in explanations for the strengths they spot (Step 2).
- Offer each person a concrete deadline (set in the near future, like say "please send it back to me by this weekend" or "by Monday"). That way it doesn't get placed on the back-burner and you'll have plenty of time to assemble the feedback and reflect on it prior to Session 6 (especially for those in a live MBSP group).
- Remind people that there are no wrong answers – it is their perception of the strengths they **most strongly perceive** in you.
- Many people ask responders to limit the feedback to the **top 5 strengths** they spot in you.
- Distribute this activity in different life domains – your family, your friends, your work colleagues, your neighbors, your fellow students – in order to get a diverse picture of yourself across settings.
- Don't let humility get in the way. It's important to learn about your strengths from others so ask them about their views (it might surprise you).
- Consider letting people know that you're happy to give them strengths feedback as well!

Mindfulness-Based Strengths Practice (MBSP)
Practice Worksheet 5.1: Character Strengths 360

Step 1

Below are 24 character strengths. Which of these *most strongly* describes who this person is and how they operate in their life? Check off the 5 strengths that you *most clearly* see in them (limiting your responses to 5 provides more power and meaning to what you select and will help the person in compiling the feedback from multiple people). Be sure to provide examples for each in Step 2.

___ **Creativity:** ingenuity; sees & does things in new and unique ways; has original & adaptive ideas

___ **Curiosity:** novelty seeker; takes an interest; open to different experiences; asks questions

___ **Judgment:** critical thinker; analytical; logical; thinks things through

___ **Love of learning:** masters new skills & topics; passionate about knowledge & learning

___ **Perspective:** wise; provides wise counsel; sees the big picture; integrates others' views

___ **Bravery:** valorous; does not shrink from fear; speaks up for what's right

___ **Perseverance:** persistent; industrious; overcomes obstacles; finishes what is started

___ **Honesty:** integrity; truthful; authentic

___ **Zest:** enthusiastic; energetic; vital; feels alive and activated

___ **Love:** gives and accepts love; genuine; values close relations with others

___ **Kindness:** generous; nurturing; caring; compassionate; altruistic; nice & friendly

___ **Social intelligence:** aware of the motives and feelings of self & others, knows what makes other people tick

___ **Teamwork:** a team player; community focused, socially responsible; loyal

___ **Fairness:** acts upon principles of justice; does not allow feelings to bias decisions about others

___ **Leadership:** organizes group activities; encourages and leads groups to get things done

___ **Forgiveness:** merciful; accepts others' shortcomings; gives people a second chance

___ **Humility:** modest; lets accomplishments speak for themselves; focuses on others

___ **Prudence:** careful; wisely cautious; thinks before speaking or acting; does not take undue risks

___ **Self-regulation:** self-controlled; disciplined; manages impulses & emotions

___ **Appreciation of beauty and excellence:** experiences awe; quickly moved to wonder; marvels at beauty & greatness

___ **Gratitude:** thankful for the good; expresses thanks; feels blessed

___ **Hope:** optimistic; future-minded; has a positive outlook

___ **Humor:** playful; enjoys joking and bringing smiles to others; lighthearted

___ **Spirituality:** purpose- & meaning-driven; has coherent beliefs about the universe; practices spiritual practices such as yoga, meditation, prayer, contemplation, sacred readings

Step 2

Important: Give a brief rationale or example of how you have seen this person display *each strength* you checked off.

Mindfulness-Based Strengths Practice (MBSP) Practice Worksheet 5.2: Character Strengths 360 Tracking Grid											
Name of Person:											
Domain (Work, Home, School, Social):											
VIA Character Strengths (spotted)										**Total:**	*Your VIA Survey Results*
1	Creativity										
2	Curiosity										
3	Judgment										
4	Love of Learning										
5	Perspective										
6	Bravery										
7	Perseverance										
8	Honesty										
9	Zest										
10	Love										
11	Kindness										
12	Social Intelligence										
13	Teamwork										
14	Fairness										
15	Leadership										
16	Forgiveness										
17	Humility										
18	Prudence										
19	Self-Regulation										
20	Appreciation of Beauty & Excellence										
21	Gratitude										
22	Hope										
23	Humor										
24	Spirituality										

Practice Activity 5.2: Character Strengths Brainstorm

Choose one character strength. What does it look like?

_____

_____

What does it mean to have or express this strength?

_____

_____

What happens if you have too little (underuse of this strength)?

_____

_____

What happens if you have too much (overuse of this strength)?

_____

_____

When and where can you use this strength in your daily life?

_____

_____

What benefits does the strength bring to you and others?

_____

_____

Write about the strength in _six words_ without including the word itself. Two examples for curiosity include: "I open doors to unknown things" and "The art of making good questions."

_____

_____

Session 6:
Mindfulness of the Golden Mean

Character cannot be developed in ease and quiet.
Only through experience of trial and suffering can
the soul be strengthened, ambition inspired, and success achieved.

Helen Keller

A story to remember

Circles can be vicious or virtuous.

Jamar was helping a nonprofit organization who hired him because they wanted a strengths-based approach to help them become more cohesive and productive as a team and with the children and adults they helped. Jamar invited the group to look at each member's character strengths on the VIA Survey. They connected closely when they spotted the strengths of one another. Things were progressing nicely as the strengths-spotting led the group members to express things they had often felt and noticed but never actually shared or appreciated in one another.

Then, Jamar asked the group to share something about one of their clients that challenged them. The team agreed that a teenager name Brittany was the most challenging to them.

One member began: "Brittany is very defiant. She disagrees with everything that we say and advise."

Another agreed: "That's true. And, I asked her to help me the other day by greeting people at the front desk. The next thing I know she was fighting with another client and had broken one of the pictures on our wall!"

"And, yesterday," began another teammate, "Brittany was running around the building yelling, singing, and just being loud. We couldn't get any of our work done!"

Jamar asked the group to pause for a moment. Brittany certainly sounded like a difficult person. He found himself thinking quite negatively about Brittany and her behaviors. He knew, from his mindfulness and character strengths training, that there was more to the person than what they showed on the surface and more than the negatives that others say about them. He knew there was always more.

After a mindful pause, he spoke again to the group. "Thank you for sharing your observations about Brittany. It sounds like there are many challenges she presents. Let me ask you this. What do you like about Brittany? What is best about her?"

"Well," began one member cautiously, "she is quite good at organizing activities. The other day she got six other clients together to play a couple of games."

"Yeah," another spoke up, "when I had asked her to help me greet people, she actually did quite a good job at the greeting part – she was friendly and engaging with every new person. She made others laugh and feel comfortable."

"The other day when I was complimenting Brittany, she was quick to point out the good qualities of other clients," said another team member.

Jamar observed the process happening on the team: "I'm noticing you are spotting a number of Brittany's character strengths – her leadership, her social intelligence, and humility. These are wonderful character strengths to observe, and you are doing a good job of seeing the behaviors connected with them. The other thing I want to point out is that when one staff member saw something negative, this appeared to cascade to another negative, and then another negative. Soon we were all caught up in it. But this vicious circle quickly shifted to a virtuous or positive circle. When one person spotted and discussed a positive quality or behavior of Brittany's, this seemed to naturally lead to another teammate seeing and discussing a character strength. And then another!"

The Power of Strengths Reframing

Brittany as described in A Story to Remember posed a challenge to every person on a helping team. The team members felt distressed and emotionally affected by her. Yet, they also had within them the capacity to reframe the situation – to see the potential, the good, the other side of what the negative mindset was showing.

All of us can learn to take a similar approach. You can see that strengths use is not just for times when things are going well and smooth. Your strengths awareness and use is equally for difficult situations and when you are with people you don't get along with. Now that your mindfulness practice is getting stronger, you're likely seeing character strengths pop up more in your conversations and actions as well. You might be mindful when your child is performing an act of kindness, when your colleague is showing perseverance in trying to help a new client, or when your relationship partner is displaying curiosity by asking you questions. Each of these examples falls within a larger dimension of your life, such as family, work, relationships, community, and so forth.

In this session, you will learn about and practice mindful strengths use in three ways:

1. You'll bring your mindful strengths use into specific situations in the different domains of your life.
2. You'll identify overuse and underuse of your character strengths, and you'll discover the optimal use of your strengths.
3. You'll learn ways to use mindfulness and character strengths to face, manage, and/or overcome problems, bad habits, and life challenges.

Together, these will offer you a more complete perspective on how to bring character strengths to your life with energy and clarity.

Your Mindful Strengths Use in Different Settings

Your strengths are expressed *situationally.* That is, you show up with your strengths differently in the various scenarios that make up your work life, home life, and social life. And your use of them will also vary by degrees in different settings. Some situations call for one of your lower strengths, whereas others require a stronger use of your signature strengths. There is plenty to take notice of – and it's mindful awareness that makes all the difference in our lives.

You might find it easy, for instance, to express curiosity at work but discover that you really don't use that same kind of exploratory questioning approach with your family members. Or you might notice that you're quick to be loving, warm, and genuine at home but struggle with appropriate expression at work. Each area of your life and each situation may call for different strengths to be brought forth. Take a moment to open up your mindfulness to notice this in yourself.

Name a character strength – any strength – that you'd like to focus on.

_____

Choose three settings from the following list, then explore how you currently use this strength in each of them: work; school; family; parenting; intimate relationship; social life; sports; hobbies; spiritual community; volunteer community; social networking community; neighborhood.

Setting #1: _____

How you use the strength:

_____

_____

_____

_____

Setting #2: _____

How you use the strength:

_____

_____

_____

_____

Setting #3: _____

How you use the strength:

_____

_____

_____

_____

Which setting was easiest for you to explore? Did examples and insights about your strengths use in that setting seem to flow from you? In which setting did you have the most trouble coming up with ways you use the strength? What obstacles do you notice?

_____

_____

_____

Many people find that there is a gap, a discrepancy, in the degree to which they express a strength in one setting as opposed to another. And yet maintaining a fair amount of consistency in how strengths are expressed – that is, having a smaller gap across settings – is associated with greater well-being. Take a look at your 24 strengths, searching for discrepancies. For example, perhaps you express creativity well as a soccer coach but not in your relationship with your spouse. Once you notice this, you can mindfully bridge the gap – you can use the strength of curiosity to find new ways to apply creativity to your relationship, or you can use the strength of social intelligence to consider the needs of your partner and then find creative ways to support those needs.

? What discrepancy in your strengths use do you notice? How might you use a different strength to bring balance or close this gap?

_____

_____

_____

_____

? Return to the list of settings above. In which setting would you like to be more engaged or connected? What character strength(s), especially signature strengths, might you bring forth to become more engaged in this setting? How might you do that?

Setting: _____

Character strength(s): _____

How you use the strength:

_____

_____

_____

_____

? How might mindful awareness support you in your character strengths use?

_____

_____

_____

You've explored how contexts or settings matter in terms of your character strengths use. You've discovered the crucial role of mindfulness in supporting these insights. Now is the perfect time to take the next step of looking at the nuances of situations and interactions with others in which you overuse or underuse your strengths.

> **YOUR MINDFUL PAUSE**
>
> Pause for a moment. Close your eyes and breathe for 15 seconds. Focus only on your in-breath and your out-breath.
>
> Ask yourself: *Which of my character strengths might I bring forth right now?*
>
> Take action with the character strength that rises strongest within you. This might be an action in your thinking, your words, or your actions – right now, or in your near future.

Overuse and Underuse of Strengths

Any of the 24 character strengths can play out too strongly or too lightly (or not at all). If you were to use a mindful microscope to closely examine your strengths use - or lack thereof - in your various life situations you would discover that it is very common to use too much of a particular strength in some situations (strength overuse) and too little of a strength in others (strength underuse).

When is it too much or too little? The answer is simple: when you are negatively impacting yourself or another person by your overuse or underuse.

This means there is a subjective level – an interpretation – by you and by others as to whether or not you are overplaying or underplaying a strength. And subjectivity can be tricky to deal with. So how can you accurately assess your own strengths use?

The first step is to become mindful that we are potentially overusing or underusing our strengths. Most of the time, we are partly or completely unaware of our strength overuse and underuse. So just bringing mindfulness energy to our possible overuse or underuse is sometimes sufficient to transform a situation or lead us to action. In other words, simply being mindful of this issue sets us on a path of positive change toward *optimal use* – the desired balance between overuse and underuse.

Ideally, we might aim for optimal strengths use when possible – what's known as the *golden mean* of character strengths use. In this strengths zone between too much (overuse) and too little (underuse), we pursue the right combination of our strengths, expressed at the right intensity, and fit for the situation.

The openness and acceptance implicit in mindful awareness allows you to honestly examine the boundaries of where your optimal use ends and your overuse or underuse begins. Sometimes, of course, there's not a perfect spot in the zone, as there may be several optimal uses of various strengths in a particular situation. But if you stay the course of pursuing the golden mean, you can take action in the moment as best you can and then later reflect on how things turned out or gather feedback from others.

The strengths continuum shown in Figure 1 illustrates this. The further we go to the right *or* the left side, the more we slide into autopilot mode, in which we're not mindfully using our strengths. Habitual underuse can emerge as inattentiveness, being unaware or unreflective, seeming lazy or negligent. Habitual overuse can emerge as being forceful, heavy-handed, narrow-minded. It's up to each of us to apply mindfulness to discover what's *just right* for a particular situation given our own personality, who we're with, and what's going on around us.

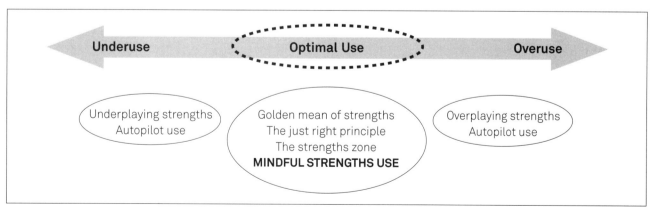

Figure 1.   Strengths continuum from underuse, to optimal use, to overuse.

Learning about overuse and underuse can be enhanced by understanding the language of overuse and underuse. What is the overuse of fairness? What's the underuse of prudence? How might we find a balance with a given strength? Box 3 shows the overuse, underuse, and mindful use (optimal use) of each of the 24 character strengths. After this, the following three sections offer practical approaches to working with overuse, underuse, and optimal-use of your strengths.

Box 3. Language for overuse, underuse, and mindful use of 24 character strengths

Overuse: eccentric, odd, scattered
Creativity: original, clever, imaginative, unique, and practical
Underuse: conforming, unimaginative, plain or dull

Overuse: nosy, intrusive, self-serving
Curiosity: "explorer," intrigued, open, novelty seeker
Underuse: bored, uninterested, apathetic, self-involved

Overuse: lost in the head, narrow-minded, cynical, rigid, indecisive
Judgment/critical thinking: analytical, detail oriented, open-minded, rational, logical
Underuse: illogical, naïve, unreflective, closed-minded

Overuse: know-it-all, elitist, overwhelming
Love of learning: information seeker, lifelong learner
Underuse: Smug; complacent with knowledge or growth; uninterested

Overuse: overbearing, arrogant, disconnected
Perspective: wise, wider view, integrator
Underuse: shallow, superficial, lacking confidence

Overuse: risk taking, foolish, overconfident, unconcerned regarding others' reactions
Bravery: valorous, facing fears, confronting adversity
Underuse: cowardly, unwilling to act, unwilling to be vulnerable

Overuse: stubborn, obsessive, fixated
Perseverance: persistent, gritty, task completion
Underuse: lazy, helpless, giving up

Overuse: self-righteous, rude, inconsiderate
Honesty: truth sharer and seeker, sincere, without pretense, authentic
Underuse: phony, dishonest, inauthentic, lacking integrity

Overuse: hyperactive, overactive, annoying
Zest: energized, enthusiastic, happy, active
Underuse: sloth-like, passive, sedentary, tired

Overuse: emotional overkill; misaligned with others' needs; sugary sweet or touchy-feely
Love: warm, genuine, connected, relational fulfillment
Underuse: isolating, cut off from others, afraid to care, not relating

Overuse: intrusive, compassion fatigue, overly focused on others
Kindness: compassion, care, generous, nice and friendly
Underuse: indifferent, selfish, uncaring to yourself, mean-spirited

Overuse: over-analytical, self-deception, overly sensitive
Social intelligence: empathic, tuned in then savvy, knowing what makes people tick
Underuse: clueless, disconnected, naiveté, emotionally insensitive

Overuse: dependent; lost in groupthink, blind obedience, loss of individuality
Teamwork: collaborative, participative, loyal, socially responsible
Underuse: self-serving, individualistic, going it alone

Overuse: detached, indecisive on justice issues, uncaring justice
Fairness: equality for all, care and justice-based, moral reflection
Underuse: prejudice, partisanship, complacency

Overuse: bossy, controlling, authoritarian
Leadership: positive influence, organizing a group, leading around a vision
Underuse: follower; compliant and mousy; passive

Overuse: permissive, doormat, too lenient or soft
Forgiveness: letting go of hurt when wronged, giver of second chances, mercy, accepting shortcomings
Underuse: vengeful, merciless, easily triggered

Overuse: self-deprecation, limited self-image, subservient, withholding about oneself
Humility: modesty, clear view of oneself, focus attention on others, sees own limitations
Underuse: arrogant, braggadocio, self-focused, heavy ego needs

Overuse: stuffy, prudish, rigid, passive
Prudence: wise caution, thinks before speaks, planful, goal-oriented, risk manager
Underuse: thrill seeking, reckless, acting before thinking

Overuse: constricted, inhibited, tightly wound, obsessive
Self-regulation: self-management, mindful, disciplined
Underuse: self-indulgent, emotional dysregulation, impulsive, undisciplined, unfocused

Overuse: snobbery, perfectionistic, intolerant, unrelenting standards
Appreciation of beauty and excellence: awe, wonder, elevation, admiring, seeing the life behind things, experiencing beauty and greatness
Underuse: oblivious, autopilot, mindlessness

Overuse: ingratiation, contrived, profuse, repetitive
Gratitude: thankful, connected, appreciating the good and positive
Underuse: unappreciative, entitled, self-absorbed

Overuse: unrealistic, Pollyanna-ish, head in the clouds, blind optimism
Hope: optimistic, positive expectations, confidence in goals and future
Underuse: negative, pessimistic, past oriented, despair

Overuse: tasteless or offensive, giddy, socially inappropriate
Humor: playful, funny, laughing with others, seeing the lighter side
Underuse: overly serious, stilted or stiff, flat affect

Overuse: proselytizing or preachy, fanatical, rigid values, holier than thou, narrow-minded
Spirituality: connecting with the sacred, finding purpose and meaning, expressing virtues
Underuse: lack of purpose or meaning in life, disconnected from what is sacred, unaware of core values, uncaring toward various forms of life

Note. Adapted from Niemiec (2019).

Explore Overuse of Your Strengths

Overuse of strengths may take many forms, such as forcing yourself to forgive someone when you are not ready, or unintentionally bringing too much humor to your efforts to support a friend who is struggling with a loss. You might overthink a decision – overusing judgment/critical thinking – that leaves you confused and in a state of indecisiveness, or your appreciation of beauty and excellence might drive you to unrealistic standards and perfectionism.

You can certainly overuse any of your 24 strengths, but odds are you are more likely to overplay your highest character strengths, because these come so easily to you. Sometimes you bring these strengths with a *force*, and you might not be aware that you are doing that. In addition, it's easy to take these strengths for granted (using them on autopilot). At times, it *is* helpful to use your strengths without

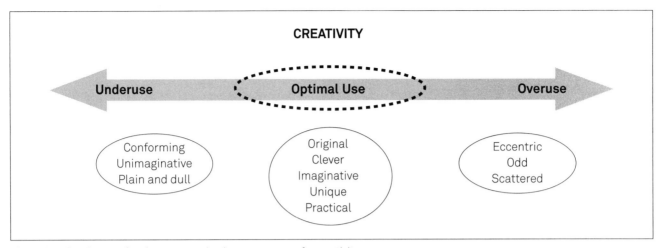

Figure 2.   Continuum of underuse, to optimal use, to overuse, for creativity.

even trying, but at other times, it can come across as too much. Without mindful attention to your strengths use, automatic use of your strengths may end up appearing reactive, self-serving, inappropriate, or simply imbalanced. This can have a negative effect on others.

Let's take a look at your two highest strengths on the VIA Survey. Write those two strengths here:

_____   _____

Next, you will create a strengths continuum for each of these two strengths, so you can examine how the overuse and underuse of these strengths might come across. Figure 2 offers an example for creativity.

Please fill in the strengths continuum for the first strength you wrote down. Be sure to use Box 3 to help you with the language.

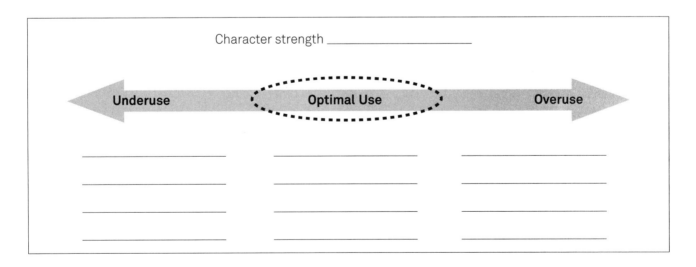

? What strikes you about this continuum? What resonates most strongly for you?

_____

_____

_____

_____

? When do you tend to overuse this strength? In which settings are you most likely to overuse it? Around which people in your life do you overplay the strength? Explore your patterns here.

_____

_____

_____

_____

? Is there one story that highlights when you overused this strength? Think about that for a moment. Share it here.

_____

_____

_____

_____

? Although you will explore this later, take a moment to reflect on times when you have _underused_ this strength. When have you come up short with this strength? When are you most likely to _not_ bring forth this important signature strength?

_____

_____

_____

_____

Repeat this process with the other strength you wrote down.

Character strength _____

Underuse   Optimal Use   Overuse

_____   _____   _____

_____   _____   _____

_____   _____   _____

_____   _____   _____

? What strikes you about this continuum? What resonates most strongly for you?

_____

_____

_____

_____

? When do you tend to overuse this strength? In which settings are you most likely to overuse it? Around which people in your life do you overplay the strength? Explore your patterns here.

_____

_____

_____

_____

? Is there one story that highlights when you overused this strength? Think about that for a moment. Share it here.

_____

_____

_____

_____

? Although you will explore this later, take a moment to reflect on times when you have *underused* this strength. When have you come up short with this strength? When are you most likely to *not* bring forth this important signature strength?

_____

_____

_____

_____

From Overuse to Optimal Use

As you explored your tendencies to overuse some of your strengths above, did you wonder about how to find more balance? About what optimal use might look like for you?

For the first strength you've been working on, consider a situation in which you used the strength in an optimal way. First, read the example below of optimal strengths use for the strength of curiosity. There is not one way that strengths can be used optimally as there are infinite situations we can be in. This example may help you foster your thinking about optimal use.

Curiosity – example of optimal strengths use: Imagine you are curious about the life of someone with whom you are having a conversation with for the first time. You are intrigued by them, by their story. You are interested in knowing what they think, feel, and have done. You ask them questions and give them time to share their responses. You reciprocate with your own stories and responses, in order to keep some balance in the conversation. You realize that although questions are a good way to connect with someone, not all questions are appropriate in this situation. As you continue talking, some thoughts pop up that seem a bit random and out of place. Out of curiosity, you share one or two of these to gather

this person's opinions and impressions of these topics. With other people, in other situations, you might pause around now, change the subject, or conclude the conversation by saying you'd like to talk some more at a later date. But as the conversation with this person continues to be engaging, you realize you want to keep it going with additional exploring and sharing. To keep the engagement level high, you notice an elevation in your creativity as you come up with new talking points, as well as expression of your love of learning as you dig deeper into each area. You're aware of your zest and hope as you contemplate a future friendship with this person. Your strengths of perspective and prudence offer a balance to your curiosity as you see the bigger picture of the value of building new connections while also acknowledging that it takes time, effort, and, to some degree, caution and reflection.

Optimal strengths use involves finding one's balance with strengths use that fits right in the situation. This scenario displays the pursuit of balance in oneself (one's own comfort level) and with the person one is with (in the conversation). It also shows the natural impact and elevation of other character strengths that occurs. With this example in mind, let's turn to the first strength you wrote about in the previous section.

? With the 1st character strength you wrote about in the previous section in mind, what is a situation in which you used the strength in an optimal way? What was happening? How were you expressing the strength?

_____

_____

_____

? What character strengths tend to go along this strength when you use it optimally? How do these strengths combine in a positive way for you?

_____

_____

_____

? When you overuse this strength, what strength might help you balance or temper the overuse? Name an example of this _tempering effect_.

_____

_____

_____

? Now explore the 2nd strength you wrote in the previous section. What is a situation in which you used the strength in an optimal way? What was happening? How were you expressing the strength?

_____

_____

_____

? What character strengths tend to go along this strength when you use it optimally? How do these strengths combine in a positive way for you?

_____

_____

_____

? When you overuse this strength, what strength might help you balance or temper the overuse? Name an example of this _tempering effect_.

_____

_____

_____

Explore and Build Underused Strengths

Sometimes our underuse of strengths is just an oversight – it just never occurred to us to apply the strength of love, for example, to a community group meeting or to bring forth humility at the dinner table. We can also underuse a strength when it has faded or eroded over time, perhaps because there's little opportunity to practice it – in a rigid work environment, for example, that does not value creativity, or in an intense college class that doesn't encourage humor and playfulness.

Your strengths profile can offer you places to start exploring your underuse, just as it did for your overuse. And although *any* of the 24 strengths can be underused (including your signature strengths), let's turn for now to the most obvious candidates: those strengths at the bottom of your profile. These are strengths that you are less accustomed to using or are not practiced in using. They are particularly vulnerable to underuse because you likely don't see these strengths in yourself to the same degree that you see your top strengths.

Let's take a look at your two lowest strengths on the VIA Survey. Write those two strengths here:

_____   _____

Please fill in the strengths continuum for the first strength you wrote down. Be sure to use Box 3 to help you with the language.

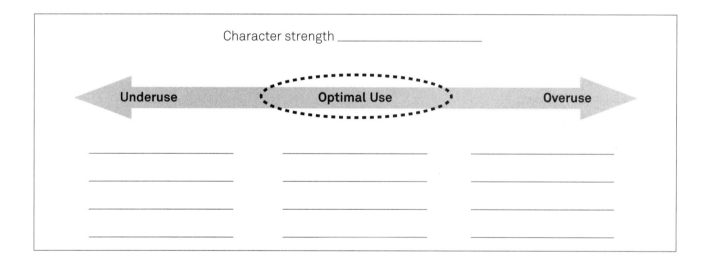

Character strength _____

Underuse   Optimal Use   Overuse

? What strikes you about this continuum for this strength?

_____

_____

Name a situation in which you brought forth too little of this strength, and you would like to use it more in future. It might be a situation in which you've routinely underused this strength or have only occasionally underused it.

_____

_____

? Which of your five highest (signature) strengths can you use to give this strength a boost? How might you do that in the situation you described? Is this optimal strength use?

_____

_____

Repeat this process with the other strength you wrote down.

Character strength _____

Underuse   Optimal Use   Overuse

_____   _____   _____
_____   _____   _____
_____   _____   _____
_____   _____   _____

> **?** What strikes you about this continuum for this strength?
>
> _____
>
> _____
>
> Name a situation in which you brought forth too little of this strength, and you would like to use it more in future. It might be a situation in which you've routinely underused this strength or have only occasionally underused it.
>
> _____
>
> _____
>
> **?** Which of your five highest (signature) strengths can you use to give this strength a boost? How might you do that in the situation you described? Is this optimal strength use?
>
> _____
>
> _____

DID YOU KNOW?

Research has found that character strengths overuse and underuse are associated with higher rates of depression, less flourishing, and less life satisfaction. Optimal use, on the other hand, is connected to higher flourishing and life satisfaction and lower depression (Freidlin et al., 2017; Littman-Ovadia & Freidlin, 2019). That is an argument for finding balance in your *strengths zone* in every situation.

Now that you've brought mindful awareness and greater balance to some of your top and bottom strengths, you're armed with a solid approach to mindfully explore and express all of your other character strengths. If you'd like to delve deeper into overuse, underuse, and optimal use, a great resource is Ryan Niemiec and Robert Mc-Grath's book *The Power of Character Strengths: Appreciate and Ignite Your Positive Personality* (2019).

Remember, there is no "perfect" use. Rather, the areas of strengths overuse, underuse, and optimal use offer you an opportunity to understand yourself through a different lens and bring the best of yourself forward in a new way. This week's exercises, which include the Fresh Look Meditation (Audio Track 10), the Mindful Pause (Audio Track 11), and From Mindless to Mindful (Practice Activity 6.1), will support you in doing that.

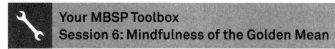

Your MBSP Toolbox
Session 6: Mindfulness of the Golden Mean

Key Insights

- *Mindful strengths use* means to bring attention to your best qualities and to use them in an optimal way that is tuned into the situation you are in.

- A *virtuous circle* can be created when one character strength expressed causes another person to express a character strength. This, in turn, might unfold back and forth and/or extend to other people.

- Character strengths are expressed situationally, showing up in different ways in different contexts, such as work, home, and social life.

- In any situation, a character strength can be brought forth too strongly (overused) or too lightly (underused). When the right amount of a strength(s) is brought forth in a particular situation, this is mindful strengths use and finding the golden mean for that situation.

From the Science

- Research has found that character strengths overuse and underuse are associated with less flourishing and life satisfaction and greater depression (and underuse is typically worse than overuse), while optimal use of character strengths is associated with higher levels of flourishing and life satisfaction and less depression (Freidlin et al., 2017).

For Your Exploration

- In which settings are you most likely to overuse one of your highest strengths? Around which people in your life do you overplay this strength? Which character strength might help you temper or balance this overused strength?

- What is a situation in which you routinely underuse one of your character strengths? Which character strength might help you boost it up?

Pearl of Wisdom

- While you can consider the lens of strengths overuse/underuse with any problem, conflict, or stressor, it should be viewed as an interpretation or a perspective for the situation, not a perfect answer or remedy, and not a replacement of purely calling out the strengths in a person.

Expand Your Toolbox

- Fresh-Look Meditation (Audio Track 10): This practice will help you reframe a problem or challenge in your life using the lens of strengths use, strengths overuse, and strengths underuse.

- From Mindless to Mindful (Practice Activity 6.1): This activity will help you understand one of your bad habits and what might be underlying it.

Mindfulness-Based Strengths Practice (MBSP)
Activities and Tracking Sheet: Session 6

Suggested Activities for This Week
- Fresh-Look Meditation (Audio Track 10), ×1/day (Audio Track 10).
- The Mindful Pause (Audio Track 11), as needed.
- From Mindless to Mindful (Practice Activity 6.1): Choose an area of your life where mindlessness has a negative impact. Practice bringing mindfulness and strengths to this area each day this week.
- Track your mindfulness and strengths experiences in this tracking sheet.

Day & date	Type of practice & time length	Obstacles to my practice	Strengths used	Observations & comments
Monday Date:				
Tuesday Date:				
Wednesday Date:				
Thursday Date:				
Friday Date:				
Saturday Date:				
Sunday Date:				

Audio Activities for Session 6

Track 10: Fresh-Look Meditation

The Fresh-Look Meditation is a particularly powerful exercise due to the main concepts it taps – reframing, dealing with problems, observing overuse, observing underuse, grounding oneself with mindfulness and one's breath anchor, practicing nonavoidance of problems, and bringing forth signature strengths or other strengths for a transformative effect. You'll be invited to imagine a small problem or minor stressor in detail, to welcome and be open to the thoughts and emotions that are present as you imagine it. You'll then have an opportunity to reflect on strengths you might be underusing or overusing with this problem and a way to take a different perspective. It's useful to consider what small problem you will focus on prior to beginning the meditation. Do you have a minor problem in mind that you'd like to work on?

Track 11: The Mindful Pause

You'll notice this practice has been embedded in each chapter of this Workbook. Now you have the opportunity to listen to this short, highly applicable activity in audio form and bring it into your daily life as a practice!

Practice Activities for Session 6

Practice Activity 6.1. From Mindless to Mindful: Shifting One of Your Problems or Bad Habits

We all have to deal with problems, stressors, and conflicts. Many stem from our own bad habits or vices that have become mindless patterns that trap us. No doubt you can identify a habit or difficulty you'd like to change. Whether it's late-night snacking, drinking too much, or overreacting with anger, each of us has improvements we can make. Rather than trying to make a dramatic change, we can use our mindfulness and strengths to shift our focus and learn about ourselves.

In this activity, you'll shift your attention from an entrenched, challenging habit, to the underlying autopilot aspect of it. It will not only help you transition from mindlessness to mindfulness, it will also transition you from strengths overuse/underuse to optimal use.

Steps

1. Select one of your bad habits or vices that you are bothered by and would like to change. Choose something you are currently struggling with on an almost daily basis.
   Examples: taking second or third helpings at dinner, staying up too late, arguing with your partner, constantly complaining about a particular person, yelling at your children, spending too much time on social media, biting your nails, driving too fast, watching too much television, or being overly critical of others.
2. The next time you engage in this habit, observe your experience closely. Rather than trying to change the bad habit, focus on your autopilot mind instead. What was going through your mind right before you engaged in the habit? What is your autopilot mind saying as the habit unfolds?
   Examples: distorted thinking patterns like *I can't ever change, I'm hopeless,* or *I'm a failure;* difficult emotions like frustration, anxiety, fear, sadness, disappointment, shame, or guilt. The possibilities of what you might be thinking and feeling are virtually endless.
3. Bring mindfulness to yourself on autopilot. Deliberately practice mindful breathing and self-observation during the habit. Continue bringing mindful attention to the experience, seeing it in a fresh light.
4. What character strengths are you underusing and overusing while you engage in this habit? It's likely a combination of any of the 24, occurring in various degrees.
   Examples: too little self-regulation (discipline and self-control), too much prudence (planning), overuse of critical thinking (harsh judgments of yourself), overuse of curiosity (distracting yourself), underuse of love or fairness to yourself.
5. Which character strengths might you bring forth to become more mindful or to take action with your mindful learnings?
   Examples: bravery can help you take action with one of your mindful insights; curious questioning throughout the experience can help you understand it differently; creativity can lead you to think about the habit in new ways; kindness or forgiveness can be granted to yourself during the undesirable behavior.

The worksheet on the next page will help you look more closely at your experience to help you deepen your understanding and facilitate growth.

Name the habit or vice you wish to target.

_____

? What goes through your mind right before you engage in the habit? What does your autopilot mind say as the habit unfolds? When does your mind tend to wander off during the habit?

_____

_____

_____

_____

_____

? What character strengths are you underusing and overusing while you engage in this habit?

_____

_____

_____

_____

? Which character strengths might you bring forth to become more mindful or to take action with your mindful learnings? How will you do this?

_____

_____

_____

_____

_____

Session 7:
Authenticity and Goodness

The most authentic thing about us is our capacity to create, to overcome, to endure, to transform, to love and to be greater than our suffering.

Ben Okri

A story to remember

One day early in 2022, I had a rough start to the day. I had just learned school was cancelled for the week, and so my wife and I – both working full-time – would have to somehow manage our three children throughout the upcoming workdays. Apparently, these young children need food, water, and lots of attention! Then, we learned that one, maybe two, of them were sick, and so we needed to now find a way to get them to the doctor (and they could not be seen together by the doctor due to a COVID protocol, so we'd have to make the trip to the doctor on two separate occasions, as soon as possible). As the stressors piled up, so did my frustrations. I became reactive and started in on a pity party as I complained to my wife about anything I could think of.

The tension mounted as I thought about meetings I had that day, people waiting to hear back from me on projects, articles I needed to write, and research I needed to conduct.

Mindful of my upset feelings and thoughts, I turned to my strength of perspective. I gave myself the advice: "Ryan, go walk the dog." I listened. As I stepped out of my home environment of triggers, tension, and crying kids, I immediately began to let go (i.e., forgiveness). My walk become infused with greater mindfulness as I walked through my woods and neighborhood with more zest and appreciation of beauty. I found some of my hope and prudence strengths and planned out how this new day might look and with a sudden newfound optimism, I texted my wife, "It will all be OK."

I returned ready to take on the day and the stressors that would undoubtedly unfold.

The next hour, while driving my daughter to the doctor, I spilled not only my water but also my coffee (usually I just spill one). Yes, I do enjoy having open cups in my car as opposed to sealed containers. The coffee perfectly pooled up in my plastic, squared console a half-inch deep. My 6-year-old daughter observed this new (and quite novel) pool of coffee that had formed a liquid square:

"Wow, look at that!" she exclaimed with pure delight, despite her sore throat and headache.

"That's really cool," I noted as I marveled at the black square. "I will need to soak that up with some napkins I have in the glovebox."

"Oh, can you just leave it there? I like looking at it."

"It is interesting to look at, isn't it? But each time I am turning the car, the pool slowly spills over onto the floor. So, I better clean it up."

"OK."

The rest of the day plodded along from the doctor's visit, medication pickup, work meetings, writings, kids' activities, and some nighttime reading and tai chi. No more reactivity; stressors handled as they came. One day later, I looked back at the previous day. At a glance, nothing stood out as remarkable.

My summary was something like: It started out difficult and things turned out all right.

But later that day I had the opportunity to closely examine the day with a wise person who has great listening skills. She helped me to see the day anew.

Here's the new summary of the day:
- When I went to evaluate myself, I was drawn immediately to "what went wrong" and I gave my greatest attention to my early reactivity and frustrations of the morning. The picture of the day was colored with this reactivity.
- The vicious circle that flows from stress to upsetting thoughts and feelings, to more stress and back around again can be shifted. We can create a virtuous circle flowing from mindfulness to one character strength to another strength to deeper mindful attention and back around again. For me, mindfulness led to forgiveness to love to hope to creativity and so on throughout the day. The virtuous circle started by using one character strength in a mindful way. That buffered me from later challenges, surprises, and difficulties.
- More frequently than I would give myself credit for, I was operating at a presence level or mindfulness approach, such as the naming of the tension in the moment, the presence with my daughter, and the deliberate use of different strengths at challenging moments.
- In looking at the day more deeply, I understood I was doing better than I realized. I was using more character strengths than I realized. Mindful responsiveness and character strengths were ever-present opportunities at any moment.
- All of these insights would likely have been lost if it hadn't been for deeper reflection and also a mindful conversation.

Be True, Do Good

The previous story offers some interesting nuggets to consider on our mindfulness and strengths journey:
- Character strengths use emerges gradually, then suddenly.
- From the chaos, there is mindfulness and strengths use.
- Stress unfolds and seems to take over the mind, but if there is a moment left in the day, there is a moment left for character strengths use.
- Look deeply: You are probably doing better than you think you are doing.

Consider some of the most popular, well-worn phrases that personal inspiration authors use and that have resonated with people for decades. What comes to mind? "Be all that you can be," "Stay true to yourself," "Believe in yourself," and "Do good for others," to name only a few.

The underlying themes of so many of these books and messages seems to boil down largely to two key words: "authenticity" and "goodness." In the language of character strengths, this would be expressed as something like "Be authentic by being true to who you are, to your core strengths," and "express goodness to others and the world by using your core strengths." In a nutshell: Be yourself and do good.

These concepts have been central to your work in each session of this Workbook thus far. When you combine mindful attention and mindful living with your character strengths, you rediscover your best qualities and then make your relationships and the world a little bit better each time you use them.

Authenticity – being true means to know who you are, to know your strengths, and to act consistently from those qualities (mostly what's referred to here as your *signature strengths*). Those who express their signature strengths in a balanced way across the domains of their life are commonly labeled as comfortable in their own skin, and they don't allow others or society to tell them otherwise. Authenticity is linked with simply learning to be, and mindfulness helps bring our strengths forward in a balanced way. This is the *being* of human nature. As the popular mindfulness teacher Jon Kabat-Zinn often advises, we need to learn how to bring the *being* back into *human being*.

Goodness – doing good means to use all of our character strengths – each of the best qualities that are at our disposal – for the greater good. The *greater good* might be equivalent to being more wise and compassionate to others and to the world – to bring ourselves forward as a "positive contribution" to others and our planet. It might take the form of community activism, careful, mindful listening to someone who is suffering, teaching or leading people to use their character strengths, or using our character strengths to improve the lives of the people we know and meet. Strengths can be used not just for thinking and perspective shifting, but they're also for *doing* – doing kind and fair and brave and humble acts to benefit others in all kinds of ways. This is the *doing* of human nature, learning to be good at being a human doer by means of your whole repertoire of character strengths.

There is certainly an interconnection between authenticity and goodness, between being and doing. In many situations, one directly leads to the other, and in other situations they are expressed simultaneously. Yet they can also be viewed as separate entry points to improving ourselves. While both might matter to you, it's likely that one speaks to you more for some reason. Let's explore this further.

> Which do you find yourself drawn to more strongly at this period of your life: **authenticity**, learning to *just* be and consistently deploying your signature strengths while doing so, or **goodness**, striving to *do good* for others and the world, working regularly to bring forth and elevate your character strengths? Explain your response below.
>
> _____
>
> _____
>
> _____
>
> _____
>
> Keep your findings here in mind as you progress through this session. We'll be referring to this idea again later.

Strengths Branding

Let's try an experiment, an activity called *strengths branding*. Not unlike a company that captures what is unique and special about its product with a brand name, color, phrase, and/or symbol, we will practice branding with our strengths! Your character strengths are special to you, and their combination with mindful awareness brings that uniqueness to the next level. Strengths branding helps to solidify and elevate that reality as well as help you advance the strength further in your life. Let's try it.

Start by choosing one of your signature strengths. Consider choosing the strength that you think best describes who you are.

_____

Now merge the word "mindful" or "mindfully" with the character strength you selected. For example, "mindful gratitude" or "mindfully grateful" or "mindfully fair" or "mindful fairness." This is the start to your personal brand, like your own personal tagline!

_____

Make note of how your brand can serve your authenticity (getting better at _being you_) or your goodness (doing more good in the world), whichever you chose above. As you bring mindful attention to authenticity and goodness, how might this align with your branding?

_____

_____

Next, think about how this merging of mindfulness and character strengths is who you are and how you wish to express yourself in the world. Consider how your brand inspires your actions at home with your family, at work, during difficult moments, and during regular routines. It's useful to start this statement with something like, "I brand myself with [fill in your tagline] because …" Incorporate your own strongest mindfulness elements as well as mindfulness overall into your response.

_____

_____

_____

_____

_____

_____

_____

_____

You've now got a new tool with which to _be_ and _do_ in the world! Keep your strength brand top of mind from now on to inform your plans and goals for using your mindfulness and character strengths.

YOUR MINDFUL PAUSE

Pause for a moment. Close your eyes and breathe for 15 seconds. Focus only on your in-breath and your out-breath.

Ask yourself: *Which of my character strengths might I bring forth right now?*

Take action with the character strength that rises strongest within you. This might be an action in your thinking, your words, or your actions - right now, or in your near future.

Mindful Goal Setting and Strengths Planning

In this Workbook, you've been discovering your signature strengths and your strongest mindfulness qualities. You've begun to explore and reflect on each and to take positive actions with them. You've focused on applying mindfulness and character strengths to many of your relationships, to your stressors, bad habits, and life challenges, and to activities and routines of daily living. You've examined, in a practical way, how your mindfulness impacts your character strengths expressions, as well as how strengths can be infused to help you sustain a stronger and more mindful living practice.

With the four questions that follow, consider all of your work far. Also consider what might be possible for your future. Each area of reflection attempts to cut to the heart of the matter. No doubt, each offers potential for substantial depth of contemplation, but for now, be brief in your responses, trying to sum up your thoughts in just a sentence or two.

1. What matters most to you? In this one life that you have, what matters most to you?

_____

_____

2. Imagine for a moment you are lying on your deathbed and reflecting on your life. Complete this sentence:

"I wish I had spent more time _____ "

3. Look to your future. Imagine you see a positive experience involving your mindfulness and character strengths use. What comes to your mind? What's the first thing (e.g., person, place, situation) that pops up?

_____

_____

4. Think about your reflections earlier in this session on authenticity and/or goodness. What is the most important part of your mindfulness and strengths practice to help you stay strong on the path of authenticity and/or goodness?

_____

_____

_____

Together, all of the reflecting you've been doing, questions you've been answering, and experiments you've been conducting have been forming the foundation of your *mindful goal setting*. Goal setting that is done with mindfulness and character strengths is filled with meaning, vitality, and very direct personalization for you. Rather than a typical goal someone sets, such as to exercise more or eat healthier, mindful goal setting is based on your deepest values and sense of purpose. It gathers up all the mindfulness and strengths wisdom you have procured in your life up to this point and puts it into action by creating a conscious plan for moving forward.

To make a personal action plan for you, start by reviewing all of your responses in this session, to remind yourself what is most meaningful to you. Then set two specific goals for your immediate future that will relate to and be supported by planned activities, character strengths, and mindfulness. Example of a specific goal: *I want to continue my daily practice of mindfulness each morning and increase the time to 12 minutes per day, or I want to spot and appreciate character strengths in at least three people each day.*

Goal #1

_____

_____

This goal, like any goal, requires simple actionable steps you must take to make it a reality. What things can you actually *do* to start working toward this goal? For example, *I will set my timer to wake up each morning for my mindfulness practice, or I will write down the strengths I spotted and appreciated in people in a notepad that I'll keep by my bed before going to sleep each night.*

Activities

_____

_____

_____

_____

_____

Character strengths serve as a natural energy source driving you to reach the goal you have set and to fulfill the activities you have listed. Which of your signature strengths and other character strengths will be most important to bring forth here? For example: *I will use my signature strength of gratitude during each morning meditation to keep me motivated and to start my day off strong.* Or, *I will use my perspective to actively spot strengths in people at work, and I'll use my curiosity to ask people in my community questions that will encourage them to speak about their strengths.*

Character Strengths

_____

_____

_____

_____

_____

Your mindfulness energy and attention provides another pathway for reaching goals and fulfilling activities. How might mindfulness help support your goal? For example, *During my practice of gratitude, when I get distracted, I'll use my senses to keep me grounded in the experience.* Or, *When I'm strengths-spotting, I'll use mindfulness to describe the qualities and nuances of each strength I spot in others.*

Mindfulness

_____

_____

_____

_____

_____

What step are you ready to take toward your goal right now, however small?

_____

_____

Goal #2

_____

_____

Activities

_____

_____

_____

_____

_____

_____

Character strengths

_____

_____

_____

_____

_____

Mindfulness

_____

_____

_____

_____

_____

What step are you ready to take toward your goal right now, however small?

_____

_____

_____

_____

_____

More Tips for Setting Effective Goals

1. Frame goals positively. Focus on what you want to achieve rather than what you want to get rid of.
2. Be as specific as you can with each step in the process. It's helpful to note things that are measurable rather than general.
3. Choose things that are clearly within your control and doable. For example, it is probably too vague to say, "I want to be happier." Instead, say, "I want to take two actionable steps to boost my happiness each day." You have control over the latter, and it is measurable and clear.
4. Consider what is realistic and within reach for you.

If you get stuck anywhere along the way in this session, feel free to jump to the meditations (the Best Possible Self, which is Audio Track 12, and the Signature Strengths Breathing Space, which is Audio Track 13) and strengths activity (Grow a Character Strength, which is Practice Activity 7.1) that conclude the chapter. These have been designed to support your work in these areas and to help you expand upon your thinking on authenticity/goodness, strengths branding, and goal setting before turning to Session 8.

 DID YOU KNOW?

In her survey research, Tasha Eurich (2018) found that 95% of people think they are self-aware, but only 10–15% truly are.

As you grow in your mindfulness practice and your character strengths awareness and use, you'll move yourself further along into clarity and depth of self-awareness.

Self-awareness is foundational for the themes of being authentic and expressing goodness.

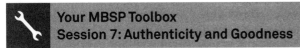

Your MBSP Toolbox
Session 7: Authenticity and Goodness

Key Insights

- Mindfulness and character strengths can emerge out of chaos, overwhelm, and suffering. Despite the stress that has unfolded in your day, if there is a moment left in the day, there is a moment left for character strengths use.
- You can bring mindfulness and character strengths to your pursuit of authenticity (knowing and being true to who you are) and goodness (doing good and bringing your best to improve the world). For example, you can make an effort to live your life from your signature strengths (authenticity) and you can make an effort to bring forth many/any of your 24 strengths for the greater good (goodness)

From the Science

- Research has shown that while a majority of people believe they are self-aware, only a minority truly are (Eurich, 2018). We need to remind ourselves that we all have plenty of growth to be fostered and taking a humble approach to ourselves might be particularly helpful for that growth.

For Your Exploration

- Are you drawn more to the pursuit of authenticity or the pursuit of goodness in your life? How might you express your strengths to support this part of your journey?

Pearl of Wisdom

- *Being* authentic and *doing* good are not mutually exclusive. One can lead to the other. Generally, it is useful to start by wholeheartedly focusing on one which can naturally support the other.

Expand Your Toolbox

- Experiment with the strengths branding activity described in this session.
- Set a goal in which character strengths are the means (pathway) for achieving the goal or they are the ends (the goal itself).
- Best Possible Self Meditation (Audio Track 12): Consider your best possible self at a particular future time-point, and as you image it, name the character strengths that will be pathways to help you reach it.
- Grow a Character Strength (Practice Activity 7.1): Choose any of your 24 character strengths to build up by using the aware, explore, apply model.

Mindfulness-Based Strengths Practice (MBSP)
Activities and Tracking Sheet: Session 7

Suggested Activities for This Week

- Meditation of your choice, ×1/day (practice what you are curious to learn more about or engage with your most energizing, joyful practice).
- Listen to the Best Possible Self activity (Audio Track 12) at least one time this week.
- Signature Strengths Breathing Space meditation (Audio Track 13), ×1/day.
- Grow a Character Strength with the aware-explore-apply model (Practice Activity 7.1)
- Meaningful Photo Activity (Practice Activity 7.2).
- Track your mindfulness practices, including mindful walking, eating, driving, etc., here or in your journal.

Day & date	Type of practice & time length	Obstacles to my practice	Strengths used	Observations & comments
Monday Date:				
Tuesday Date:				
Wednesday Date:				
Thursday Date:				
Friday Date:				
Saturday Date:				
Sunday Date:				

Audio Activities for Session 7

Track 12: Best Possible Self Meditation

This exercise involves two basic steps: visualizing yourself at a future moment in time having accomplished your goals, and considering the character strengths you'll need to deploy to make that vision a reality. This activity involves visualizing your best possible self in a way that is very pleasing to you and that you are interested in – really seeing this "future you" in close details. It could involve your best possible self in general, your best possible self in relationships, your best possible self at work, or a different domain. You might think of this as reaching your full potential, hitting an important milestone, or realizing one of your life dreams. The point is not to think of unrealistic fantasies, but rather of something that is positive and attainable. Then, after you have a fairly clear image, you'll ask yourself: What character strengths will be my key pathways to reaching my best possible self?

Track 13: Signature Strengths Breathing Space

The Signature Strengths Breathing Space meditation brings together a variety of ideas from previous weeks and the current session – the application of signature strengths, the use of gathas, using the breathing space, and the aware-explore-apply model. This exercise also highlights one of the most important takeaways: bringing greater awareness to the nuances and uses of your signature strengths.

Practice Activities for Session 7

Practice Activity 7.1. Grow a Character Strength

Building up any of your 24 character strengths is easier than you think! Use the research-supported *aware-explore-apply* model below as your guide. These three steps provide the framework and direction for you to grow any of your strengths.

1. Aware

The first step of any change process is awareness. Bring your awareness to the language of the 24 character strengths. Think about how much or how little you bring forth each strength, as you review the 24 concepts and definitions.

What character strength do you *want* to grow? What character strength do you *need* to grow?

In this step, mindfulness helps you shift from autopilot and strengths blindness to a place of greater awareness and readiness for strengths development.

Which character strength will you focus on? _____

Reflections on this **aware** phase:

_____

_____

_____

_____

_____

2. Explore

The next step is to develop a deeper understanding of the character strength you selected. A first-line exploration is to reflect on how you have used this strength successfully in the past. Even though there are times when you came up short or when you brought forth too much of it, be sure to fully capture many ways you have used the strength.

Past:
- How have you used this strength to overcome stressors and life challenges? Your relationship conflicts or your personal vices?
- How have you used this strength during the best of times? Your proudest moments? During your experiences of great connection with others?

Present:
- How are you using this strength right now, as you read and reflect?
- How did you use this strength earlier today?

Future:
- How might you bring more of this strength in the future at work? At home?
- How might it serve your life goals better?

Your exploration with these questions might be points of discussion with someone, starting points for you to meditate upon, or the subject of your journaling or self-monitoring.

In this step, mindfulness helps you cultivate deeper insight into who you are and draw new connections with your past and current behaviors.

Character strength: _____

Reflections on this **explore** phase:

_____

_____

_____

_____

_____

3. Apply

The third step is the action phase. After you have spent sufficient time exploring, you are probably ready to take action with this character strength. The most common approach is to set a plan to use or cultivate this strength based on the insights you gleaned in Step 2. The plan might involve boosting the character strength or using the strength more deliberately to help you reach a life goal (such as meeting a new relationship partner or earning a work achievement).

What stands out most to you from Step 2? What action might you take? Perhaps you can set up a new routine that involves using this strength more.

In this step, mindfulness helps you stay connected to the question "What matters most?" and helps you figure out wise actions to take in that direction.

Character strength: _____

Reflections on this **apply** phase:

_____

_____

_____

_____

_____

Practice Activity 7.2: Meaningful Photo Activity

Purposes: This activity engages your mindfulness and character strengths to foster a central well-being component – that is, meaning in life. In addition, it serves as a strategy for consolidating learning and growth while building perspective around your mindfulness and character strengths journey. (For those in an MBSP group, this is a fun and substantive way to connect with the group.)

Research: This activity is based on research with students who took several meaningful photos and then reviewed and described them, which led to increases in life meaning, positive emotions, and life satisfaction (Steger et al., 2013). In the study, the most common meaningful photos were of relationships, hobbies and leisure, and nature.

Steps for the activity

1. Use your mindfulness and character strengths to reflect on something personally meaningful, life giving, or insight generating from your mindfulness and character strengths journey in this workbook so far.
2. Take a photo (it is OK to take more than one) that attempts to capture this meaning. It may involve people, environment, symbolic items, and/or other representations.
3. Sit with the photo and savor it. Consider printing it and placing it somewhere you can see it regularly. Share it with family/friends. (If you are part of a Mindfulness-Based Strengths Practice (MBSP) group, share it with your fellow participants or leader, as appropriate.)

Session 8:
Your Engagement With Life

Some people die at 25 and aren't buried until 75.

Benjamin Franklin

I am unable to make the days longer, so I strive to make them better.

Henry David Thoreau

A story to remember

Can a stranger's smile impact you for an indefinite period of time?

I was on a meditation retreat in a large group that was engaging in an activity together. I felt the need to step away for a moment, so I walked into one of the buildings where the meditation hall was. I went to the second floor to the sanctuary area, and I was surprised to see one person in the large space, sitting on a cushion. I walked closer to sit nearby the person, who I noticed was a large-sized man sitting quietly on a cushion with his eyes closed. He looked like the epitome of peacefulness. His peace seemed enhanced by the medium-sized smile on his face. It was a steadfast calm smile. It seemed to connote his being unwavering, solid in the moment, strong in himself.

I did not know the man and never said a word to him. I would never know if I saw him on the street, and he certainly would never know me. Yet, there was resonating impact. This is one of the examples I think of when I consider the power of smiling, and especially when I think of the importance of practicing smiling while practicing mindfulness – any kind of mindfulness. For someone like me who has humor as a low strength, smiling is particularly important.

This was something so simple, so easy to take for granted. How could it stick with me for decades? It was not special or remarkable and is now faded and distant, but there was lasting impact.

A Pathway Toward Growth

The peaceful smile of the stranger shows the impact that we can have on others – and never know it – in small ways. Consider then, the power of the mindful listening you give to someone, or the modeling of your fairness, creativity, or gratitude at a community meeting or work event. Even the most subtle actions – and any moment of mindfulness – has the potential to be transformative. It starts with us using our mindfulness and character strengths to engage with the present moment – to engage with life.

This final session invites you to engage with life in many ways. One way is to examine your work in this Workbook so far in the context of progress toward your goals, and how you will keep this progress going in the months ahead. This is referred to as *maintenance toward growth* – keeping your momentum in motion, continuing to grow and make progress, and adapting as needed.

Keeping Up With Your Goals

? How are things going with your mindfulness and strengths goals and practices so far?

_____

_____

_____

_____

_____

? What positive gains have you noticed? What have you learned from both your successes and obstacles on this journey?

_____

_____

_____

_____

_____

? Take a look at the photo you took for the Meaningful Photo Activity in Session 7. What strikes you most now as you revisit the photo? This photo captured something particularly meaningful about your mindfulness and character strengths journey. How might this wisdom inform your goals moving forward?

_____

_____

_____

_____

_____

? What is the most important message you could provide yourself with right now to inspire you to persevere and keep up with your goals?

_____

_____

_____

_____

_____

? Who might support you in keeping up with your goals? Is there someone who will participate in one of the goals or activities with you? Are there one or two people you can regularly talk to about your plan – do a "check-in" with? Are there people you think would be good cheerleaders for you, asking how things are going and supporting you along the way? Who will you call on for assistance, and how would you like them to support you?

_____

_____

_____

_____

_____

Cues are external reminders that bring you back to remembering your goals and practicing with them. A cue might be as simple as setting a chair in a certain place so you'll see it and practice mindfulness on it. Or it could be a whiteboard in your house that lists your goals, or a phone app that helps you track your progress. It could be a _mindfulness bell_ you set to go off randomly on your computer, or Post-It notes positioned in different places in your home or office to bring you back to thinking about your goals.

How might you weave in cues to support you in the long run? Identify some cues here:

Cue 1 _____

Cue 2 _____

Cue 3 _____

Staying Motivated

Your reflections in the previous section will be important for keeping you strong on your goals. That said, everyone has difficulties with keeping up with their goals, from time to time. Everyone. Therefore, it can be useful to know what scientists refer to as the *stages of change* (Table 2). If you are mindful of these five stages, you can quickly catch yourself when you slip from one of your goals, and you can pull yourself back to where you want to be. These stages can also help guide you toward new behavior change and to help others make changes!

Table 2. Five stages of change

Stage of change	Explanation around mindfulness or strengths	Self-talk	Action to move forward
Precontemplation	"I don't see a value or reason to work on strengths or practice mindfulness."	"I'm not going to do any practice." "I can't build my strengths. I can't be mindful – it's too hard!" "I don't know how mindfulness could help me." "I don't know how to use my strengths and don't care to know."	Read about any character strength. Understand the *why* of strengths.
Contemplation	"I see some value in working on mindfulness and strengths, but I'm not taking any action now."	"I may work on my mindfulness in the future." "It could be important for me to set up a strengths practice someday."	Listen to stories and examples of those who successfully use mindfulness and strengths. Watch videos of strengths in action (e.g., the power of kindness, courage, or gratitude).
Preparation	"Working on mindfulness and/or strengths is important to me. I am getting ready to make a change."	"I'm reading this Workbook to get ideas to take action." "I am starting to write down my goals to start a mindfulness practice in the near future."	Engage in goal-setting practices: Make the goal and steps to reach it clear; write it down; share with those who will support you.
Action	"I have begun a strengths and/or mindfulness practice."	"I am practicing mindful walking each day." "My practice is that I'm spotting at least one character strength in each person I meet each day."	Give yourself small rewards after the action (e.g., coffee; time to surf Internet, a few minutes of creativity, etc.) Know the possible obstacles and setbacks and ways to use strengths to overcome them.
Maintenance	I have a mindfulness or strengths practice that has continued for more than 6 months.	"I feel good about my regular strengths practice." "Sticking with mindfulness each day over an extended period of time has really helped me."	Keep your practice fresh (weave in new character strengths). Fine-tune your practice to ensure ongoing learning and growth.

? Which of the five stages are you in right now with regard to your mindfulness and strengths practice?

_____

_____

_____

_____

? How might you catch yourself if you find your motivation to practice with mindfulness and strengths begins to slip?

_____

_____

_____

_____

? What is most important for you to stay motivated?

_____

_____

_____

_____

? What might be the community or group that would support you with your practice? How often will you connect with your community?

_____

_____

_____

_____

> ⏱ **YOUR MINDFUL PAUSE**
>
> Pause for a moment. Close your eyes and breathe for 15 seconds. Focus only on your in-breath and your out-breath.
>
> Ask yourself: *Which of my character strengths might I bring forth right now?*
>
> Take action with the character strength that rises strongest within you. This might be an action in your thinking, your words, or your actions - right now, or in your near future.

Engagement With Life

You have so many resources innately within you. Your capacity for strength is vast. You have already used your mindfulness and your character strengths in countless ways throughout your life. Some have been unconscious and some conscious. This Workbook is intended to help you make your usage *more* conscious and *more* impactful in your life. Over the weeks of going through this Workbook, you have become more engaged in your own life and probably in the lives of those close to you.

When you think of the word "engagement," you probably envision a person or an activity that involves some kind of commitment. Take a larger view of this from the perspective of the grand scheme of your life: What is your commitment to life? How might you be fully there for life as it happens, as much as possible?

To be mindful and strengths-based is to be engaged in the task, routine, or conversation at hand. Our engagement with life is something we can continue to grow but never perfectly achieve. It's our connection with and within any given moment.

Here are a handful of key messages to take away from this Workbook to help you reinforce your engagement with life:

- **Notice** your mind's autopilot tendencies. Embrace this capacity of your mind. *Catch your autopilot mind, as soon as possible* (Catch AP-ASAP).
- **Return** your attention back to the present moment with openness and curiosity a billion more times in your life.
- **Bring** awareness to your character strengths often; accept and value your strengths; find ways to express them regularly in your life.
- **Practice** spotting and overtly valuing the strengths of others, in good times and in difficult times.
- **View** your mindfulness practice (and the obstacles that come up) as an opportunity to deepen your connection with yourself, others, and the world.
- **Embrace** your problems by using your character strengths. Consider how you may have overused or underused your strengths in the past, and understand how you can deploy them now to temper overuse or underuse and to better manage problems.
- **Implement** goals in which you can use your strengths to help you get the most out of life.
- **Build** mindfulness and strengths into your daily routines. Continue to find new ways to express your signature strengths in your life.
- **Maintain** a mindfulness practice that resonates the most with you. Use your strengths to stick with it.
- **Revert** to a *beginner's mind* (seeing things as if for the first time) at least once every day.
- **List** a few additional key messages that have struck you.

? What are the most important takeaways for you?

_____

_____

_____

_____

_____

_____

_____

? Which of these messages is most meaningful to you?

_____

_____

_____

? What's the very next thing you will do with your mindfulness?

_____

_____

_____

? What's the very next thing you will do with your character strengths?

_____

_____

_____

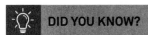

> **DID YOU KNOW?**
>
> Research has found that workers who are highly aware of their strengths are 9 times more likely to be flourishing than those with low awareness. And those reporting high use of strengths are 18 times more likely to be flourishing than their low-use colleagues. Workers reporting that they feel highly appreciated are 29 times more likely to be flourishing than those who feel less appreciated (Hone et al., 2015).
>
> These findings are offered here as good reminders of the central themes of this Workbook: strengths awareness, mindful strengths use, and strengths appreciation.

Continue your exploration and practice by taking action with the Sacred Object Meditation and stretch yourself out of your comfort zone with the strengths activity, Teach the Mindful Pause. In addition, what are your mindfulness and character strengths practices that you will regularly keep up with moving forward?

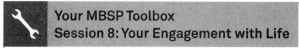

Your MBSP Toolbox
Session 8: Your Engagement with Life

Key Insights

- Your mindfulness and character strengths goals can be adjusted and improved upon, forever. They are an important part of your personal growth. They can be benefitted by support and cues. Support means to include others in your goal-setting so that you can have people to cheer you on, engage in the goal with you, or can serve as accountability for you. And, setting up cues – external reminders – can help serve as a "mindfulness bell" to wake you up from auto-pilot and bring you back to your strengths and your desire to be mindful.

- You can track (in an ongoing way) your motivation for your goals by assessing your readiness for change. Are you in a precontemplation stage, contemplation, preparation, action, or maintenance?

- When you engage with life, you connect with it. You are fully there. You can engage with life in any experience you are in.

From the Science

- In a large study, researchers found that workers who reported engaging their strengths the most were 18 times more likely to be flourishing than those workers who used their strengths least (Hone et al. 2015).

For Your Exploration

- What is the most important message you could provide yourself right now to inspire your mindfulness and character strengths goals?

- What is your commitment to "life"? How can you be fully there, with life, as it unfolds??

Pearl of Wisdom

- Select two or three pearls of wisdom or insights from anywhere in this workbook that you would like to memorize and make part of your life. Some examples include: notice my mind's autopilot tendencies each hour; catch my AP-ASAP; return my attention to the present moment with openness and curiosity; practice spotting and appreciating the strengths of others, often and regularly; embrace my problems with character strengths.

Expand Your Toolbox

- Sacred Object Meditation (Audio Track 14): Select a special object in your life that can serve as a reminder cue for your growing understanding and use of character strengths and mindfulness.

- Teach the Mindful Pause (Practice Activity 8.1): Share this practice with someone in your life. The simplicity of the steps allows this practice to be accessible and practical for virtually anyone. Who would you like to give the gift of mindfulness and character strengths to?

Mindfulness-Based Strengths Practice (MBSP) Activities and Tracking Sheet: Session 8

Suggested Activities for This Week
- Meditation of your choice, ×1/day (engage in the practice that brings you insight and joy, and that you want to use to energize and support yourself).
- Listen to the Sacred Object Meditation, at least once.
- Teach the Mindful Pause (give the gift of this simple, powerful, highly applicable practice to someone else).

Day & date	Type of practice & time length	Obstacles to my practice	Strengths used	Observations & comments
Monday Date:				
Tuesday Date:				
Wednesday Date:				
Thursday Date:				
Friday Date:				
Saturday Date:				
Sunday Date:				

Audio Activities for Session 8

Track 14: Sacred Object Meditation

This activity guides you in sanctifying an object; in other words, making it particularly special, sacred, and powerful.

You will set the object up as an ongoing cue for your mindfulness and your character strengths awareness and use. It can therefore serve as a special reminder of all your progress and growth, which you are experiencing in the present moment and continue into the future.

Practice Activities for Session 8

Practice Activity 8.1. Teach the Mindful Pause

Pay It Forward!

The fruits of your mindfulness and character strengths journey can be seen in any practice you have done. The Mindful Pause is one of those practices. You can pay it forward to those in your life you care about. You might refer to Audio Track 11 for a refresher on the Mindful Pause, and recall the times you paused in each of the Sessions of this Workbook to practice it.

In your mindfulness and character strengths journey so far, you have made small changes and perhaps big strides. You've explored mindfulness and strengths individually and together, you've experienced their synergy, and you've overcome obstacles and challenges. You've embraced a range of good and bad life experiences, and you've appreciated the good. Throughout this Workbook, you've been taught and have been invited to practice the mindful pause.

When you teach something, you have the chance to maximize your learning by sharing your knowledge and experience of it as you describe it to others, answer their questions about it, and support them with it. This week's final activity is to "pay it forward" by sharing and teaching the mindful pause to two people in your life. In doing so, you will be sharing something meaningful to you with them and bringing benefit to them as well.

Steps

1. Choose two people from any area of your life. Explain to them that you'd like to teach them a short, valuable strategy involving mindfulness and character strengths.

2. Share with them the simple steps: pausing in the moment, doing nothing but feeling their breathing in and out for 15 seconds, and posing the question to oneself at the end. Be sure to tell them about the character strengths that have arisen for you during the activity, and how and why you've found this to be an effective, useful strategy to practice daily.

Follow up with them on their experience. This might be an immediate follow-up if you practice the activity together, or it might be a follow-up a day or week later.

Tips

- For some people, this activity offers a refreshing perspective, and they're eager to do it; for others, it's a challenge.
- Explain the purpose of the activity, for example: "I've been finding a lot of benefit from a short activity that combines strengths and mindfulness. It helps me become more aware of what is going on in my mind and body. It helps me deal with my stress in a strengths-based way. Would you like to try it with me?"
- Remember to tap into your strengths to help you help them. Perhaps you'll need to call on your bravery to let go of your worries about how others will react to your request. Or your perspective strength, to help you keep in mind the bigger purpose of why you're sharing the activity. Or perhaps your curiosity will help you ask the person questions and gently explore how to make the most of the activity.

Concluding Thoughts

You have come a long way. Mindfulness and character strengths are the *work* of a lifetime. You can surely see the importance of this work for your relationships, your professional and educational aspirations, and your personal life. If you continue the practice, you'll be nurturing the seeds of this good work within you. There's no end point, only new beginnings. And you've taken the beginning steps of an exciting journey.

It's a journey on which you have mindfulness and character strengths as close companions at your side, as tools to inspire you, as strategies to overcome struggles, and as places within yourself that you can turn to – at *any* moment, of *any* day, at *any* time.

Breathe. Smile. You are here ... right now.

Notes on Supplementary Materials

The following materials for your book can be downloaded free of charge once you register on our website:

MBSP Toolboxes

Your MBSP Toolbox Session 1: Mindfulness and Autopilot

Your MBSP Toolbox Session 2: Character Strengths and Signature Strengths

Your MBSP Toolbox Session 3: Obstacles and Struggles are Opportunities

Your MBSP Toolbox Session 4: Strengthening Mindfulness in Everyday Life

Your MBSP Toolbox Session 5: Your Relationship With Yourself and Others

Your MBSP Toolbox Session 6: Mindfulness of the Golden Mean

Your MBSP Toolbox Session 7: Authenticity and Goodness

Your MBSP Toolbox Session 8: Your Engagement with Life

Mindfulness-Based Strengths Practice (MBSP) Activities and Tracking Sheets

Mindfulness-Based Strengths Practice (MBSP) Activities and Tracking Sheet: Session 1

Mindfulness-Based Strengths Practice (MBSP) Activities and Tracking Sheet: Session 2

Mindfulness-Based Strengths Practice (MBSP) Activities and Tracking Sheet: Session 3

Mindfulness-Based Strengths Practice (MBSP) Activities and Tracking Sheet: Session 4

Mindfulness-Based Strengths Practice (MBSP) Activities and Tracking Sheet: Session 5

Mindfulness-Based Strengths Practice (MBSP) Activities and Tracking Sheet: Session 6

Mindfulness-Based Strengths Practice (MBSP) Activities and Tracking Sheet: Session 7

Mindfulness-Based Strengths Practice (MBSP) Activities and Tracking Sheet: Session 8

Audio Activities

Track 1 Beginner's Mind Meditation

Track 2 Body-Mindfulness Meditation

Track 3 You at Your Best and Strengths-Spotting

Track 4 Character Strengths Breathing Space Meditation

Track 5 Mindful Breathing With Strengths Meditation (Strong Mindfulness)

Track 6 Mindful Walking Meditation

Track 7 Strengths Gatha

Track 8 Loving-Gratitude Meditation

Track 9 Strength-Exploration Meditation

Track 10 Fresh-Look Meditation

Track 11 The Mindful Pause

Track 12 Best Possible Self Meditation

Track 13 Signature Strengths Breathing Space

Track 14 Sacred Object Meditation

Practice Activities

Practice Worksheet 1.1: Mindfulness With a Routine Activity Tracking Sheet

Practice Worksheet 2.1: Use Your Signature Strengths in New Ways Tracking Sheet

Practice Worksheet 2.2: Character Strengths Fluency Builder Example

Practice Worksheet 3.1: Mindful Listening and Speaking Practice

Practice Worksheet 5.1: Character Strengths 360

Practice Worksheet 5.2: Character Strengths 360 Tracking Grid

Reading Activities

Mindfulness-Based Strengths Practice (MBSP) Reading Activity 1.1: Overview of Mindfulness-Based Strengths Practice

Mindfulness-Based Strengths Practice (MBSP) Reading Activity 2.1: VIA Fact Sheet

Mindfulness-Based Strengths Practice (MBSP) Reading Activity 2.2: VIA Classification of Character Strengths

DOWNLOAD

How to proceed:

1. Create a user account (or, if you have already one, please log in)

For customers from the USA and Canada:

hgf.io/login-us

For customers from the rest of the world:

hgf.io/login-eu

2. Download your supplementary materials

Go to My supplementary materials in your account dashboard and enter the code below. You will automatically be re-directed to the download area, where you can access and download the supplementary materials.

Code: B-DXV7VQ

To make sure you have permanent direct access to all the materials, we recommend that you download them and save them on your computer.

Resources

The World Needs You (Poem)

Note. I wrote this poem in March 2020 to inspire people early on in the COVID-19 period to stay engaged with life, to remember they have 24 qualities that can help them, and to use those qualities to make the world better, one person at a time. I believe it remains just as relevant today.

The World Needs You

The world needs your ideas, your strategies, your best coping tools (creativity).

The world needs you to talk with interest to those around you, letting them express & release their burdens (curiosity).

The world needs your rational & balanced thinking, to counterbalance the inner voices of panic and anxiety (judgment).

The world needs you to keep learning and growing, in new ways, so you can feel good about your day (love of learning).

The world needs your sound advice, a glimpse of the bigger picture amidst the scary details (perspective).

The world needs your bravery – to help someone you've never helped, to see the world anew despite fear (bravery).

The world needs you to persevere – to push through huge obstacles and suffering you've never faced before (perseverance).

The world needs your truthfulness – now is not a time for exaggeration, fake news, or guesswork (honesty).

The world needs your enthusiasm – to uplift your energy even when you feel sucked dry from uncertainty & unknown (zest).

The world needs every ounce of your warmth & genuineness now– each ounce is worth 10x its original value (love).

The world needs you to not lose sight of your compassion and generosity, or your active seeking of ways to help (kindness).

The world needs your empathy – every city, neighborhood, & being – can be a subject of your concern (social intelligence).

The world needs you to see you are a citizen of a (very) large group that can choose to be collaborative (teamwork).

The world needs your fairness – instead of hoarding, give; instead of blaming, praise; instead of the victim, the hero (fairness).

The world needs your leadership – your fresh ideas will inspire the different groups you are part of (leadership).

The world needs you to let go of the family irks, slights, and irritations that will fill your mind (forgiveness).

The world needs you to sometimes put the attention on others and not yourself (humility).

The world needs you to be cautious every time you leave home, at least for awhile (prudence).

The world needs you to be under control, not riddled with anger but contagious with your peacefulness (self-regulation).

The world needs you to feel inspired by others' goodness because that means you might be altruistic too (appreciation of beauty).

The world needs your hope and silver linings, offered thoughtfully, as so many around us are falling into cracks of darkness (hope).

The world needs your appreciation, show others you are seeing their kind acts and they will do more of them (gratitude).

The world needs your humor (!) – your playfulness, your ability to create levity when we feel heavy and frazzled (humor).

The world needs you to see we are all in this together, that every action has a preceding action and consequence (spirituality).

The world needs you. . . All of you.

Website Resources

VIA Institute on Character: https://www.viacharacter.org

- **MBSP** (take the course live and virtually with the author!)
  https://viacharacter.org/courses
- **MBSP Certification**
  https://viacharacter.org/courses
- **Mindfulness and Character Strengths Report**
  https://viacharacter.org/reports
- **Mindfulness topic**
  https://viacharacter.org/mindfulness
- **Mindfulness and Strengths in Daily Life** (on-demand, consumer course)
  https://viacharacter.org/courses

Blooming Strengths Sangha (a free mindfulness and character strengths community, open to all, in the tradition of Thich Nhat Hanh/Plum Village)

- https://bloomingstrengths.wixsite.com/blooming-strengths

VIA Strengths, on YouTube

- https://www.youtube.com/VIAStrengths

Psychology Today Blog – What Matters Most? (By Ryan Niemiec)

- https://www.psychologytoday.com/blog/what-matters-most

Thich Nhat Hanh/Plum Village

- https://plumvillage.org/

Recommended Reading

Books on Character Strengths by Ryan Niemiec

For the General Public or Consumer

The power of character strengths: Appreciate and ignite your positive personality (with Robert McGrath). 2019. VIA Institute on Character.

The positivity workbook for teens: Skills to help you increase optimism, resilience, and a growth mindset (with Goali Saedi-Bocci). 2020. New Harbinger.

The strengths-based workbook for stress relief: A character strengths approach to finding calm in the chaos of daily life. 2019. New Harbinger.

For the Practitioner

Mindfulness and character strengths: A practical guide to MBSP. 2023. Hogrefe.

Character strengths interventions: A field-guide for practitioners. 2018. Hogrefe.

For the Academic

Character strengths and peace psychology: Foundations for science and practice. 2024. Springer.

Character strengths and abilities within disabilities: Advances in science and practice (with Dan Tomasulo). 2023. Springer.

Positive psychology at the movies 2: Using films to build character strengths and well-being (with Danny Wedding). 2014. Hogrefe.

Scientific References

Note. These are the articles and sources that are mentioned directly in this Workbook, or are otherwise important for the concepts discussed. For summaries of hundreds of scientific studies on character strengths, including their connections with mindfulness, go to https://www.viacharacter.org/research/findings.

Birtwell, K., Williams, K., van Marwijk, H., Armitage, C. J., & Sheffield, D. (2019). An exploration of formal and informal mindfulness practice and associations with wellbeing. *Mindfulness, 10,* 89–99. https://doi.org/10.1007/s12671-018-0951-y

Bishop, S. R., Lau, M., Shapiro, S. L., Carlson, L., Anderson, N. D., Carmody, J., Segal, Z., Abbey, S., Speca, M., Velting, D., & Devins, G. (2004). Mindfulness: A proposed operational definition. *Clinical Psychology: Science and Practice, 11,* 230–241. https://doi.org/10.1093/clipsy.bph077

Carlson, E. N. (2013). Overcoming the barriers to self-knowledge: Mindfulness as a path to seeing yourself as you really are. *Perspectives on Psychological Science, 8*(2), 173–186.

Eurich, T. (2018, January 4). What self-awareness really is (and how to cultivate it). *Harvard Business Review.* https://hbr.org/2018/01/what-self-awareness-really-is-and-how-to-cultivate-it.

Freidlin, P., Littman-Ovadia, H., & Niemiec, R. M. (2017). Positive psychopathology: Social anxiety via character strengths underuse and overuse. *Personality and Individual Differences, 108,* 50–54. https://doi.org/10.1016/j.paid.2016.12.003

Gander, F., & Proyer, R., Ruch, W., & Wyss, T. (2013). Strength-based positive interventions: Further evidence for their potential in enhancing well-being and alleviating depression. *Journal of Happiness Studies, 14*(4), 1241–1259.

Hanley, A.W., Warner, A.R., Dehili, V.M., Canto, A. I., & Garland, E. L. (2015). Washing dishes to wash the dishes: Brief instruction in an informal mindfulness practice. *Mindfulness, 6,* 1095. https://doi.org/10.1007/s12671-014-0360-9

Hone, L. C., Jarden, A., Duncan, S., & Schofield, G. M. (2015). Flourishing in New Zealand workers: Associations with lifestyle behaviors, physical health, psychosocial, and work-related indicators. *Journal of Occupational and Environmental Medicine, 57*(9), 973–983.

Kabat-Zinn, J. (1990). *Full catastrophe living.* Dell.

Kashdan, T., Blalock, D., Young, K., Machell, K., Monfort, S., Mcknight, P., & Ferssizidis, P. (2017). Personality strengths in romantic relationships: Measuring perceptions of benefits and costs and their impact on pand relational well-being. *Psychological Assessment, 30*(2), 241–258.

Littman-Ovadia, H., & Freidlin, P. (2019). Positive psychopathology and positive functioning: OCD, flourishing and satisfaction with life through the lens of character strength underuse, overuse and optimal use. *Applied Research in Quality of Life, 15,* 529–549. https://doi.org/10.1007/s11482-018-9701-5

Nhat Hanh, T. (1979). *The miracle of mindfulness: An introduction to the practice of meditation.* Beacon.

Nhat Hanh, T. (1991). *Peace is every step.* Bantam Books.

Nhat Hanh, T. (2009). *Happiness: Essential mindfulness practices.* Parallax Press.

Niemiec, R. M. (2018). *Character strengths interventions: A field-guide for practitioners.* Hogrefe.

Niemiec, R. M. (2019). Finding the golden mean: The overuse, underuse, and optimal use of character strengths. *Counseling Psychology Quarterly, 32,* 453–471. https://doi.org/10.1080/09515070.2019.1617674

Niemiec, R. M., & McGrath, R. E. (2019). *The power of character strengths: Appreciate and ignite your positive personality.* VIA Institute on Character.

Niemiec, R. M., & Pearce, R. (2021). The practice of character strengths: Unifying definitions, principles, and exploration of what's soaring, emerging, and ripe with potential in science and in practice. *Frontiers in Psychology, 11,* Article 590220. https://doi.org/10.3389/fpsyg.2020.590220

Oliver, M. (2017). *Devotions: The selected poems of Mary Oliver.* Penguin.

Peterson, C., & Seligman, M. E. P. (2004). *Character strengths and virtues: A handbook and classification.* Oxford University Press; American Psychological Association.

Prochaska, J., & DiClemente, C. (1983). Stages and processes of self-change of smoking: Toward an integrative model of change. *Journal of Consulting and Clinical Psychology, 51*(3), 390–395. https://doi.org/10.1037/0022-006X.51.3.390

Proyer, R. T., Ruch, W., & Buschor, C. (2013). Testing strengths-based interventions: A preliminary study on the effectiveness of a program targeting curiosity, gratitude, hope, humor, and zest for enhancing life satisfaction. *Journal of Happiness Studies, 14*(1), 275–292. https://doi.org/10.1007/s10902-012-9331-9

Salzberg, S. (1995). *Lovingkindness: The revolutionary art of happiness.* Shambhala.

Schutte, N. S., & Malouff, J. M. (2019). The impact of signature character strengths interventions: A metaanalysis. *Journal of Happiness Studies, 20,* 1179–1196. https://doi.org/10.1007/s10902-018-9990-2

Segal, Z. V., Williams, J. M. G. & Teasdale, J. D. (2002). *Mindfulness-based cognitive therapy for depression: A new approach to preventing relapse.* Guilford Press.

Steger, M., Shim, Y., Barenz, J., & Shin, J. Y. (2013). Through the windows of the soul: A pilot study using photography to enhance meaning in life. *Journal of Contextual Behavioral Science, 3*(1), 27–30. https://doi.org/10.1016/j.jcbs.2013.11.002

About the VIA Institute

The mission of the VIA Institute on Character is short, yet complex: to advance the science and practice of character strengths.

Based in Cincinnati, Ohio, USA, the VIA Institute on Character is a non-profit organization dedicated to bringing the science of character strengths to the world. It creates and validates surveys of character and related constructs; conducts science to expand the breadth and depth of character strengths understanding, exploration, and application; supports hundreds of researchers per year by providing measurement tools and resources (https://www.viacharacter.org/research); offers a range of education materials (courses, tailored reports, videos, and practices); and develops practical strengths-based tools for individuals and professionals, such as counselors, managers, and educators (https://www.viacharacter.org/professionals).

Core to the VIA Institute is the belief that the rigorous, scientific pursuit to understand the range and dimensions of human goodness (e.g., character strengths) is the key to generating discoveries and strategies for improving the human experience that will enable and encourage the development and use of tools, practices, and methodologies which will fundamentally shift the trajectory of humankind toward the better.

Historically speaking, in the early 2000s, the VIA Institute supported pivotal work on the nature of positive character. A 3-year, 55-scientist investigation across the globe, led by Drs. Christopher Peterson and Martin Seligman, culminated in the landmark text Character Strengths and Virtues: A Handbook and Classification (https://www.viacharacter.org/character-strengths-and-virtues). The project also involved the creation of two valid and free measurement tools – the VIA Inventory of Strengths (colloquially known as the VIA Survey) for adults and the VIA Youth Survey.

By early 2023, there were over 30 million VIA Survey takers, 52 translations available for the adults, 28 translations available for youth, over 900 research studies summarized on character strengths on the VIA site, and 195 countries (all) where the VIA Survey had been taken.

While "VIA" [vee-uh] once stood for "Values in Action" (Values in Action Inventory; Values in Action Institute, Values in Action Classification), the name was changed in 2006 to more precisely reflect the organization's work. VIA is a word in Latin that means "the path" or "the way" and serves as a bridging word. Indeed, the VIA character strengths have been shown scientifically to be pathways to greater well-being, better relationships and health, and to managing stress and adversity. At the same time, this work offers a bridge for science and practice and a bridge to help the general public lead more fulfilling lives.

Pages for Your Own Personal Notes